FBI SNITCHES, BLACKMAIL, AND OBSCENE ETHICS AT THE SUPREME COURT

PLUS: HOW IT TOOK THIRTEEN YEARS AND THREE FOIA LAWSUITS TO GET THE FBI'S SECRET SUPREME COURT SEX AND INFORMANT FILES

By

ALEX CHARNS

Copyright 2024 M. Alexander Charns

Bull City Law Publishing (March 8, 2024, Edition)

ALEX CHARNS

Dedicated to all those who seek redress of their constitutional grievances before the Supreme Court of the United States and are not billionaires who vacation with a justice . . .

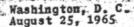
Washington, D. C.
August 25, 1965

Mr. J. Edgar Hoover
Director
Federal Bureau of Investigation
Washington, D. C.

Dear Mr. Hoover:

On July 23, 1965, under the caption "Homosexuals in the Government," this office forwarded letterhead memoranda to the Bureau setting forth information received

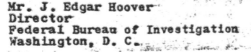

PREFACE

The thousands of FBI files about the Supreme Court that were used to write this book were never intended to be seen by anyone outside Bureau headquarters. They had no valid national security or law enforcement purpose. They were proof of the FBI's secret war on the Court. This battle, a counterintelligence program, was designed to remake the High Court in Director J. Edgar Hoover's conservative image.[1]

The FBI hid these files from the Senate Select Committee to Study Governmental Operations with Respect to Intelligence (the Church Committee) investigators in 1976.[2] They evaded releasing these files in response to a comprehensive Freedom of Information Act (FOIA) request from *New York Times* reporter Israel Shenker in 1977.[3] They told me in 1983 that no documents were responsive to my FOIA request for files on the Supreme Court. Once I proved, with their own records, that wasn't true, I sued the FBI in federal court.[4]

Chapters 1 through 4 describe the sexual blackmail of a sitting justice. Chapters 5 through 8 describe the use of the same sitting Supreme Court justice and three high-level court employees as

Bureau informants. This associate justice committed the most egregious violation of judicial ethics and betrayal of trust in Supreme Court history. Chapter 9 details the requests I made under the FOIA for FBI documents about the High Court and its justices, and the ensuing successful FOIA litigation. The book concludes with an FBI document appendix.

CHAPTER 1: SEXUAL BLACKMAIL

FBI Director J. Edgar Hoover was a self-appointed moral arbiter, America's crime fighting Cerberus; a White Anglo-Saxon Presbyterian warrior against sin. In 1925, he established a policy in which his special agents were tasked with the responsibility to forward information about "obscene and indecent" activities of "any nature whatsoever." The mailings to FBI headquarters were secretly added to the "Obscene file." Hoover's private stash of pornographic literature and movies expanded to include agents collecting the details of sexual activities of public and elected figures.[5] This might come from informers or from the FBI's illegal warrantless burglaries, wiretaps, or bugs. Hoover was a life-long bachelor. He was rumored to be the long-time gay lover of his constant companion, Clyde Tolson, his second in command. This charge was refuted by those who worked closely with the two men.[6] Hoover required his agents to report anyone who made gay allegations against him, and agents were punished for failing to do so. Hoover retaliated against his accusers. He was particularly vicious toward persons he believed were gay.[7]

Hoover also had a "Sex Deviates" program collecting "information on people suspected of being gay and passed it on to government agencies and, sometimes, the news media. The FBI had a network of informants, including doctors, helping alert the authorities to what was seen as a growing national security threat."[8]

The director had final authority whether to release his collection of tawdry sexual details to friendly reporters and destroy a career or to discreetly provide it to the subject of the scandal and turn them into a source of information or favors.[9] Hoover and his subordinates were no strangers to the game of sex, sleaze, and slime. In an infamous example, Bureau officials had attempted earlier to brand the Rev. Martin Luther King, Jr., as a "sexual degenerate." After an anonymous FBI threat did not silence King, surveillance transcripts were leaked to the press, but nobody in the media would publish them.[10]

When Hoover received damaging personal information about a prominent person, he "discreetly conveyed his reassurance to [them] that [it] would be forever locked in his bosom." As [former deputy FBI director William] Sullivan put it: "From that time on [he] would be in Hoover's pocket."[11]

The most high-profile victim of this indirect sexual blackmail was liberal Supreme Court Justice Abe Fortas.

> 7/20/67
>
> Attached memorandum from the Washington Field Office reflects possible homosexual activities on the part of Justice Abe Fortas.
>
> Messrs. Tolson and DeLoach recommend that a memorandum be prepared forwarding this information to the Attorney General.
>
> CDD:CSH

CHAPTER 2: A "RELIABLE" INFORMANT

On July 20, 1967, FBI director J. Edgar Hoover received a bombshell memorandum from the Washington Field Office. Their source in the gay community was a twenty-eight-year-old informant, "an active and aggressive homosexual," who had provided the FBI with "a great deal of reliable information" over the previous four years. His control agent was told the source of information about Abe Fortas was a young man the informer met through William Bartlett, Arnold and Porter's law firm office manager (Fortas' former firm until 1965). Bartlett had introduced George[12] to Fortas. The twenty-one-year-old George told the informant that "he had 'balled' with Abe Fortas on several occasions prior to Mr. Fortas' becoming a Justice of the United States Supreme Court." The informant, whose name is censored – redacted - from the memo, "stated that to 'ball' is to have a homosexual relationship with another male."[13]

In 1964, George was eighteen years old. His criminal record shows an arrest in 1964 for "disorderly," used as police shorthand for gay sex, illegal at the time. [14] The Metropolitan Police Department, Washington, DC record does not report a final disposition of the charge. Another version of the FBI memo about this incident shows Fortas' accuser had paid a ten dollar fine rather than go to trial. George's occupation is listed as "laborer." The next page of the FOIA release, two redactions the size of a mug shot or DMV photo, was withheld on (b)7(C) ground of privacy.[15]

Hoover's second and third in command, Clyde Tolson and Cartha DeLoach recommended that this information be forwarded to the Attorney General. If George was a minor, that would be the appropriate thing to do. The Justice Department could advise the FBI about further investigation. The Attorney General was not advised. Instead, Hoover hand wrote at the bottom of this memo: "No. DeLoach should see Fortas."

Fortas, a politically connected and talented attorney, had been married since 1935 to Carolyn E. Agger, another brilliant Yale Law educated attorney. Agger was "a tiny dynamo of a woman who smoked cigars, championed rights for women."[16] Hoover considered Fortas a "screwball" and a "sniveling liberal" as well as useful to the Bureau.[17] Justice Abe Fortas, Memphis born and raised, was the most pro-President Johnson man on the court or probably anywhere else for that matter. Their friendship began in the late 1930s when they were brought together by New Dealers William Douglas and Tommy Corcoran. One justice who served with Fortas described him as "sitting in Lyndon Johnson's lap." Justice Fortas sometimes behaved like a son, trying to please his father, even though Fortas, possibly one of the most brilliant legal minds to serve on the court, was clearly intellectually superior. Other times the tall boisterous, foul-mouthed, Texan president and the slightly built, softer spoken, and refined Jewish lawyer acted like brothers. Fortas played the violin. LBJ told crude jokes.

Fortas was a 1965 addition to the court, and he had worked with the DeLoach and the FBI before at the behest of Johnson. Fortas was the attorney who had successfully argued the *Gideon v. Wainwright*[18] case in the Supreme Court, establishing the right of indigent criminal defendants to lawyers paid by the state. The FBI had compiled thousands of pages of records over the years, describing Fortas' left-leaning friends, clients, and former membership in groups such as the National Lawyers Guild. During Fortas's days at Yale Law School, the FBI had recorded his "acquaintances" as considering him "a liberal but not a communist." In the 1940s and 50s Fortas' legal advice had been picked up in the FBI wiretaps and bugs directed at the allegedly subversive clients of his law firm, Arnold, Fortas and Porter. But DeLoach, FBI Liaison to the White House, was friendly with Fortas. Hoover trusted DeLoach's judgment. Justice Brennan remembered that Fortas was "very close to Lyndon Johnson, and close to J. Edgar Hoover. They used Fortas for a lot of things."[19]

When Johnson aide Walter Jenkins was arrested in 1964 for allegedly making gay advances to a man in the basement of a YMCA, it was DeLoach and Fortas who were called in for damage control.[20]

On July 24, 1967, at 5:10 p.m., DeLoach met Justice Fortas at his home. DeLoach told Fortas that Hoover had received "information reflecting participation in homosexual activities on his part." The Director, DeLoach said, "wanted this matter discreetly and informally brought to his attention." He assured Fortas "that the FBI was taking no further action in connection with this matter and that the fact that the Director was making this available to him was strictly for his own personal protection and knowledge."[21]

DeLoach, the former Stetson college football quarterback

who offered "reporters the chance to listen to tapes of Dr. King having sex with a woman who was not his wife,"[22] handed the one-page memo to Fortas. Fortas said the "charges were ridiculous and absolutely false." "[H]e had never committed a homosexual act in his life and while might be properly accused of normal sexual relations while a young man and during his married life, he most certainly had never committed homosexual acts at any time."[23]

Fortas said he was not surprised to learn that his law firm's thirty-three-year-old manager had been "arrested on three different occasions by the Metropolitan Police for homosexual activity." Showing the bigotry of the times, the arrest record says Bartlett's arrest was for "Disorderly Conduct - Pervert Party." The FBI informer said he knew Bartlett personally. He knew that Bartlett was "homosexual" and he had been arrested at a "gay party."

Office manager Bartlett, Fortas related, was "somewhat effeminate and that he never tried to date the girls." Bartlett supervised fifty women at the law firm. The arrest record "could certainly prove most embarrassing" to his former law firm, Fortas said, and that "something would have to be done about the situation."[24] The records do not indicate whether Bartlett was fired or whether the matter was dropped by Fortas.

Strangely, DeLoach's memo does not reflect whether Justice Fortas knew his accuser.[25] George had joked to the FBI informer that "it was convenient to have Miss Fortas on the bench." This comment might suggest George was someone who had been charged with a crime and needed help or anticipated needing legal help in the future.

DeLoach reported to Hoover in a memorandum that Justice Fortas expressed "great appreciation for having been provided" this information. "He asked that his thanks be extended to the Director for having handled the matter in this manner." The FBI memo concluded by Fortas and DeLoach discussing "the racial situation in Detroit inasmuch as Justice Fortas has been at the White House all day at the President's request, working on this matter."[26]

Hoover noted at the top-right of the memo that it was given to his personal administrative assistant Helen Gandy for filing in the "O.C.", referred to as Hoover's "Official and Confidential" files kept in his office.[27]

For the rest of Justice Fortas' ill-fated judicial career, this allegation that he had sex with a teenager remained hidden away. Even after Hoover's death in 1972 these memos were kept in a "Special File Room" at FBI headquarters. They were kept under lock and key. Almost three decades later, a photocopy of folder 71, six pages of FBI records concerning Abe Fortas, part of Hoover's "O&C" files, were brought to Greensboro, NC and handed to me in the hallway of the Federal Courthouse.

The date was July 26, 1996. My book about the FBI and the Supreme Court, *Cloak and Gavel*, had been published four years earlier. I had been told in 1983 that these FBI records did not exist.

CHAPTER 3: "DO NOT FILE" FILES

Hoover's "O&C" files contained proof of illegal FBI burglaries, warrantless wiretaps, bugging, and "derogatory personal information on two presidents, a First Lady, a cabinet member, and countless other prominent personalities." None of these records were properly indexed or recorded in the agency's central records system so high-level FBI officials could credibly testify that a search of the Bureau indices located no records.[28] The "O&C" files also included Hoover's blackmail files. Files with legitimate law enforcement or internal security purpose were indexed. Files proving FBI crimes or showing the Bureau in an unflattering light were not indexed. A failure to index files made them almost impossible to find and invisible to the outside world. It is one reason the Senate Church Committee investigators during the mid-1970s did not uncover these records about the Supreme Court and Justice Fortas.

Was this sexual allegation against Justice Fortas true? We don't know the identity of the FBI informer. Even though this accusation by George would be considered hearsay in a court of law, it is also an admission against interest of the crime of sodomy. Such an admission by George is considered trustworthy due to its associated criminal peril.

These FBI records reflect the destructiveness and pervasiveness of the "Sex Deviates" and "Homosexuals in Government" programs. No one, not even a justice on the Supreme Court, was safe from the government's vacuum cleaner of sexual scandal. Whether rumor, truth or a tall tale, the accusation had the potential to destroy careers, like those of Bartlett and Fortas.

According to Fortas biographer Laura Kalman (whose book notes do not indicate that she had access to these memos), "no one who knew of Fortas's enthusiastic heterosexuality would ever have accused him of homosexuality." According to Kalman, two influential reporters, including *Life*'s William Lambert, were told that "the FBI had a morals file on Fortas that included allegations he had once been involved in a sexual relationship with a teenage boy."[29] The reporters were told the file could be "bootlegged" out "of the FBI" for them.[30] Kalman wrote, "Regardless of the truth, such stories were damaging." If this were a reference to what was stored in Hoover's "O&C" files, only Hoover, Tolson, and DeLoach would even have known about it. It is possible that it was someone in the FBI Washington Field Office, one of the agents who supervised their informant.

According to Robert (Bobby) Baker, a disgraced political advisor to President LBJ who was convicted of tax evasion, "The interesting thing about Abe Fortas, I did not know until about 10 years ago, but a gay friend of mine, very good friend of mine, told me that Abe and his wife were both gay."[31]

Fortas' and Agger's friends thought "theirs was a marriage of minds rather than one of passion. They had separate bedrooms." And "he pursued other women" with Agger not concerned.[32]

DeLoach's autobiography does not mention anything about Fortas' sexuality or a meeting about this blackmail memo.[33] He does recount Fortas' unethical efforts to aid the FBI on illegal electronic surveillance cases pending before the Court in 1966.

The fact that a sitting Supreme Court justice knew that Hoover was keeping such a destructive secret about him – true or not – meant Fortas was beholden to Hoover.

CHAPTER 4: "SEXUAL DEVIATES"[34]

"In response to growing concern over the loyalty and security of the Federal workforce, on April 27, 1953, President Eisenhower issued Executive Order 10450 - Security requirements for Government Employment. [A]mong the list of suspect behaviors considered criminal, immoral or unethical was —sexual perversion."[35]

In 1967, being gay was considered "deviate" by some medical authorities. "Homosexuality had been listed as a 'sexual deviation' in the A.P.A.'s [American Psychiatric Association's] official Diagnostic and Statistical Manual, one of the bibles of the profession" until 1973.[36]

Justice Fortas was more progressive, seeing the humanity in this persecuted community. Only months prior to DeLoach's visit to Fortas' house, Fortas had dissented in a ruling upholding the deportation of a Canadian citizen from the U.S. because he was considered to have "psychotic personality" due to his "deviate" "homosexuality."

Justices Douglas and Fortas jointly dissented:

> It is common knowledge that, in this century homosexuals have risen high in our own public service -- both in Congress and in the Executive Branch -- and have served with distinction. It is therefore not credible that Congress wanted to deport everyone and anyone who was a sexual deviate, no matter how blameless his social conduct had been nor how creative his work nor how valuable his contribution to society. I agree with Judge Moore, dissenting below, that the legislative history should not be

read as imputing to Congress a purpose to classify under the heading "psychopathic personality" every person who had ever had a homosexual experience:

Professor Kinsey estimated that 'at least 37 percent' of the American male population has at least one homosexual experience, defined in terms of physical contact to the point of orgasm, between the beginning of adolescence and old age.

Justice Fortas had been very active in peppering the attorneys with questions during oral argument for this case, making clear his opposition to the deportation order on these grounds.[37]

In an obscenity prosecution concerning the film *Flaming Creatures* featuring some gay artistic and sexual themes, Justice Fortas was the only justice to vote to reverse the conviction.[38] The High Court's ruling was in June 1967, before DeLoach's visit. "One film critic described *Flaming Creatures* as a "faggoty stag-reel." The film was "weird and queer and made people uncomfortable." It was also called an "artistic masterpiece," influencing the work of Andy Warhol and John Waters.[39]

After the FBI informer's report, would Justice Fortas be more circumspect? To be gay or even accused of being gay in 1967 came with a heavy burden of discrimination. One could be prosecuted for sodomy, lose one's job, and be harassed. If one's sexual partner were a teenager, the results would be even more devastating to a justice in his mid-fifties or any person in a high government position.

Hoover wielded immense power over Justice Fortas. This was a threat to Fortas' future if he were considered for chief justice. It was serious enough to drive him from the Court. Fortas had to play this dangerous game with Hoover to be viewed as a valuable, reliable FBI asset. And the director had other dirt on Fortas from the year before, 1966. Dirt that Hoover wouldn't use as it was as damaging to the FBI as it was to Fortas. It was also evidence of Fortas' value and loyalty to Hoover while on the High Court. It provided a powerful reason Hoover should never use the blackmail material he possessed.

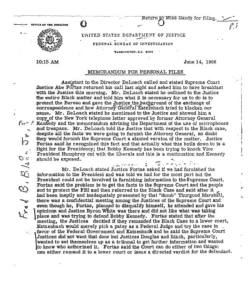

CHAPTER 5: FBI INFORMER ON THE COURT

On February 9, 1963, agents of the Federal Bureau of Investigation checked into the Sheraton Carlton hotel in Washington, DC, under assumed names. They drilled the hole in the common wall of an adjoining room and inserted a "spike" microphone through which they listen to tape-recorded conversations in the suite of Fred B. Black, Jr., next door. According to the FBI, the bug was installed to investigate whether Black had ties to racketeers. The FBI kept the microphone going for three and a half months.[40]

By 1966, the battle had begun within the executive branch over who would assume responsibility for this illegal bugging. The Black bugging had the potential of ending Hoover's career, and he knew it. To date, it was the biggest threat to his continued directorship of the FBI. Hoover needed to convince the court that former Attorney General Kennedy had authorized the bug and that Hoover was simply following orders.

Black was a quiet lobbyist, who loved horse racing as much as J. Edgar Hoover did. More important, he was a business associate of Lyndon B. Johnson's friend, Bobby Baker. Baker had been secretary to the Senate Democrats and was nicknamed "the mole" for his fast, hunched over walk. He came to the Senate as a 14-year-old page from South Carolina, studied law at night, and rose to power and influence on the coattails of his patron, Johnson. Baker's and Black's fortunes were intertwined. Both men fell from grace in political and business circles after they were sued in connection with the corrupt business practices of Serve-U Corporation, a vending machine company that placed machines in the plants of defense aerospace contractors. The Senate investigated Baker for influence peddling and obtaining contracts for the company, and later he was convicted of income tax evasion. For a brief time, Abe Fortas represented Baker, but Fortas was replaced by another all-star attorney, Edward Bennett Williams, before the case went to trial. Just as Baker's and Black's futures were joined, so were their conversations recorded in an FBI frenzy of bugging. Both men were overheard in electronic surveillance directed at their business associates.[41]

In 1964 Black was tried in federal court in Washington DC for income tax violations during the years 1956 to 1958. The prosecution's case showed that Black had received a total of $140,078 in income that he did not report. Black's defense was that his underlings had prepared his tax returns. In one instance he sent his accountant receipts for hotel expenses to be claimed as deductions, not realizing, he said, that one of his clients already paid the hotel bill for him. The jury believed the government and convicted Black, who was sentenced to between fifteen months to four years in prison and fined $10,000. Black appealed his conviction to the D.C. Circuit Court of Appeals and lost. By then Robert Kennedy had become a U.S. Senator and Nicholas Katzenbach had been appointed attorney general. On February 16, 1966, Black's attorneys filed a petition for writ of *certiorari*, lawyer jargon for a request that the Supreme Court exercise its discretionary authority to accept a case for review. Black asked the justices to overturn his conviction because, among other things, he did not receive a fair trial due to prejudicial publicity caused by the senate's investigation of Baker. One of the newspaper headlines read; "Baker associate Black goes on trial for evading $91,000 in U.S. taxes." The media called Black an "influence peddler," a description reinforced at his trial when the prosecutor, in his opening statement argued that Black was a "man who knows his way around Washington and can get things done there for his clients." Black also claimed that his constitutional rights against self-incrimination and assistance of counsel were violated when the government threatened to prosecute his former attorney who was also his friend and business partner to secure the latter's testimony against Black. His appellate attorneys wrote "it goes without saying that the use of Black's attorney as a 'Judas informer,' and star prosecution witness not only violates Black's rights under the 5th and 6th Amendments but shocks the conscience and all concepts of fairness."

A four-out-of-nine vote is required to issue a writ of *certiorari*. The Supreme Court was not impressed with Black or his lawyer's arguments. After Black petitioned the Supreme Court asking that *cert* be granted and before the justices voted on whether to accept his case, court law clerks prepared a summary called the *cert* memo with the recommendation to the justices how to proceed.

As with all such petitions, after the law clerks make the recommendations to the justices, the court meets secretly behind closed doors to vote on whether to accept the case. The conference room - the inner sanctum of the judicial temple - is situated next to the chief justice's chambers. While the justices are in conference, an employee of the Supreme Court Marshal's office stands guard outside. No secretaries or law clerks - no one other than the nine justices - are allowed inside when they take their places around the conference table and confidentially discuss and vote on each case. As Pulitzer Prize winning court reporter Anthony Lewis described it, "the conference room has a record for secrecy probably unrivaled in official Washington."

At conference on May 2, 1966, the justices voted to deny *cert* in the Black case. Black's lawyers began preparing their request for a rehearing, asking the court to reconsider its decision, even though there was no reason to believe the court would change its collective mind. But Solicitor General Thurgood Marshall was getting ready to provide a compelling reason for the Supreme Court to hear the Black case. The solicitor general, the number three man in the Justice Department, is the government's top appellate lawyer. Marshall had been instructed by his boss, Attorney General Katzenbach, to tell the court about the FBI's bugging of Black. Some conversations with Black's lawyer had been overheard. A copy of the Justice Department's (DOJ) proposed memorandum to the Supreme Court was sent to Hoover for his comments.

Angry and flabbergasted by the memo, Hoover wanted to know why the DOJ, having won the case, would give convicted tax cheat information that might allow Black to attack his conviction. Hoover objected vehemently to informing the court about the bugging, since it had nothing to do with the tax prosecution. If the court was told anything, he argued, it should be as little as possible. He also considered a number of items in the Justice Department's proposed memo to the court to be lies or deception. The draft of the DOJ's memorandum claimed that Justice Department lawyers had not known about the bugging during the trial; only the FBI had known. It was true that DOJ lawyers did not know about the bugging during Black's trial in late April and early May of 1964. On August 24, 1965, Katzenbach was told that Baker had been picked up in a "microphone ... installed at the office of Fred Black." Later that fall, Justice Department attorneys in the criminal division learned that Black's lawyer had been heard talking to Black.

Hoover instructed an assistant to meet with Justice Department attorneys to make sure that the DOJ "was not going to look like a knight in shining armor to the court and dump this whole thing on the FBI." James Gale, Hoover's emissary at the Justice Department, was successful in removing any mention or reference to the bugs placed on Black's business associates. The DOJ's memo to the court was also changed to say that the department lawyers "only recently learned that a listening device had been used." Hoover was not satisfied with these changes, believing the memorandum was still misleading.

Katzenbach wrote to Hoover explaining his reasons for making the bugging public. He and his principal advisers believed that as "officers of the court," they were "under a duty to disclose ... the fact of the inadvertent invasion of the attorney-client privilege." According to Katzenbach, "any information obtained as the result of the microphone coverage installed through trespass ... is inadmissible as evidence in court," and there was an "inescapable duty" to report the overhearing of an attorney talking to his client, even if they believe that "that it in no way affected the fairness of the trial."

Another explanation for the Justice Department's disclosure was the fear of political damage: one Senate committee was already investigating electronic surveillance - ELSUR - abuses by the federal government. The Bureau's extensive wiretapping and bugging of the Reverend Martin Luther King, Jr., had not been publicly exposed. Katzenbach had been aware of the surveillance, which, he had been told, was for the stated purpose of determining the extent of communist influence on King and on the Southern Christian Leadership Conference.

On one occasion Katzenbach had warned Hoover that these "particularly delicate surveillances" required extreme caution. The last microphone surveillance of King had been turned off during January 1966 after Hoover became afraid of what a congressional investigation might discover.

A year earlier, Attorney General Katzenbach had tightened Justice Department surveillance policies, which had formerly allowed Hoover free reign to bug and tap. The new policies required DOJ authorization for electronic eavesdropping, and a specific authorization had to be renewed every six months. Katzenbach was the first attorney general in decades to take concrete steps to reclaim from Hoover the authority to place electronic surveillances, authority that had been *de facto* surrendered to the powerful director, theoretically subordinate to the attorney general.

The microphone surveillance of Fred Black had been personally ordered by Hoover without then Attorney General Robert Kennedy's specific written or oral authorization. But Kennedy, like his predecessor attorneys general, had known that the FBI employed bugging in national security and organized crime cases and had failed to intervene because he appreciated the information obtained. Black's bugging was unrelated to Black's tax case. Hoover needed extraordinary help to escape from his predicament of being blamed for conduct that a succession of attorneys general had tacitly approved with a wink and a smile, but never in writing. The Long Committee investigations had publicized the issue of government ELSUR. But through backroom dealing, Hoover narrowly escaped congressional inquiry into the Bureau's surveillance practices.

Despite Hoover's objections, on May 24, 1966, Solicitor General Marshall[42] surprised the court when he filed an unprecedented memorandum advising the justices that: "[A]gents of the FBI installed a listening device in petitioner's hotel suite in Washington, DC. The device (not a telephone wiretap) ... was in operation for approximately two months before until approximately one month after the evidence was presented to the grand jury and indictment[43] was returned. ... During that time the monitoring agents overheard, among other conversations exchanges between [Black] and the attorney who was then representing him in connection with the tax evasion charges on which he was convicted."

The director despised Kennedy as did President Lyndon B. Johnson. Hoover did not trust Katzenbach, whom Hoover considered to be a "Kennedy man." So DeLoach recruited Fortas, a close friend and adviser to Johnson, to be his eyes and ears in the Supreme Court conference room as well as his advocate with the other justices and with the president. Justice Fortas could walk into the conference room of the U.S. Supreme Court and blame Kennedy for the bugging, thereby helping Johnson by damaging the reputation of his primary rival in the Democratic Party. The selection of the FBI-informer justice makes perfect sense when one considers Hoover's own experience with each of the justices.[44]

CHAPTER 6: G-MAN IN THE CONFERENCE ROOM

In May 1966, J. Edgar Hoover needed a Supreme Court justice to be his informer and provocateur inside the Court's oak-paneled conference room.

In the 1950s, at least three Court employees reported directly to the FBI. During the atomic spy espionage case of Julius and Ethel Rosenberg, the marshal of the court, T. Perry Lippitt, the clerk of the court, Harold B. Willey, and the captain of the Supreme court police, Philip H. Crook, kept the FBI informed about the numerous legal proceedings before the court in 1953 intended to stave off the couple's execution. Willey had even made his office and staff available to FBI agents, and suggestions were given to agents as to where to be to know immediately "what action individual [justices], or the Court as a whole, was taking." Willey and his staff also notified agents about actions "contemplated by the defense attorneys" for the Rosenbergs.

Lippitt "made arrangements for Special Agents to be ... placed in the courtroom," to enable them to be close to phones in his office from which they called headquarters with the latest information. Crook not only made his office available for the agents use, but he also "furnished ... all information heard by his men stationed throughout the Supreme Court Building. He kept Special Agents advised of the arrival and departure of persons having important roles in this case." These FBI sources of information – the clerk, the marshal, and the head of the police – were all employees of the Court. Lippitt continued to work at the Court until his retirement in 1971.[45]

Likewise, Hoover had tried to cultivate most of the justices, liberals and conservatives alike. Based on Supreme Court voting records alone, Hoover had no reason to try to approach any member of the liberal faction. Liberals were comprised of Chief Justice Earl Warren and Associate Justices Hugo Black, William O. Douglas, William Brennan, and Abe Fortas. But Hoover had access to far more than the public record on which to base his decisions. Let's consider each justice based upon what Hoover knew from FBI files.

Mr. Justice Hugo Black

In 1966 Hoover did not have a relationship with Justice Hugo Black that would allow him to ask the justice for a favor. Black, then eighty years old, had been appointed by Franklin D. Roosevelt in 1937. Roosevelt had not asked the FBI to investigate the New Deal Senator from Clay County, Alabama, but this fact did not stop the press from criticizing the Bureau when Black's former membership in the Alabama Ku Klux Klan was made public. Although the Bureau had not had much personal contact with Black, the FBI had, in the summer of 1965, laid out the red carpet and "spoiled" Justice Black's second wife, Elizabeth, and the justice's two grandsons during their "very special tour" of the Bureau. During the highlight of the visit, Hoover personally showed Mrs. Black and the children around his office, explaining the mementos and statuary that graced his office. Hoover then gave the children a Gemini and a Thor model missile from his own model collection which he kept in his outer office. Mrs. Black wrote thanking Hoover: "Dean, Jimmy, and I are at a loss for words to thank you for our fabulous time at the FBI. The crowning thrill in a day of treats, surprises, and learning came a few minutes ago when the three autographed pictures arrived by special messenger."

Unfortunately for Hoover, Mrs. Black and the boys did not

vote on the *Black* case.

Mr. Justice William J. Brennan, Jr.

Like Justice Black, William J. Brennan, Jr., President Dwight Eisenhower's 1956 nominee to the High Court, had no personal relationship with Hoover or any of his assistants. Brennan had been a justice on the New Jersey Supreme Court before his appointment. Roman Catholic, Irish, and a Democrat, Brennan was nominated by a Republican whose selection was influenced by religion, nationality, and political considerations. Brennan's appointment was supported by New Jersey Supreme Court Chief Justice Arthur T. Vanderbilt, Attorney General Herbert Brownell, and White House Appointments Secretary Bernard Shanley (an old friend of Brennan's). Although no Catholic had been on the Supreme Court since Justice Frank Murphy had died in 1949, Brennan was subjected to an impotent tirade by fellow Catholic Senator Joseph McCarthy during the confirmation proceedings. Unlike his predecessor, Justice Sherman Minton who could be counted on to support governmental actions in criminal prosecutions and loyalty/security matters, Brennan voted the opposite way. As late as 1958, Attorney General William Rogers still hoped that Brennan would pull away from the left wing of the Court-Douglas, Black, and Warren. Rogers told Hoover that he "believed ... there was a possibility ... Justice Brennan might eventually break away from the minority which holds the more extreme views." The attorney general told Hoover that greater care needed to be used in the selection of cases to take to the Supreme Court, so that Black and Douglas could not make enough of an issue of the facts of the case to turn it against the government's position. The attorney general's wishful thinking about Justice Brennan did not come to pass. Instead of moving away from Warren, Black, and Douglas, the congenial Brennan became the liberal magnet on the Court who weaved consensus out of discord.

Mr. Justice William O. Douglas

From 1937 to the late 1940s, William O. Douglas corresponded regularly with Hoover and socialized with FBI agents. In 1944 the young Justice Douglas was in such favor with Hoover that he gave the commencement speech at the FBI National Academy. A year later, Hoover trusted Douglas enough to send him confidential information regarding the Bureau's espionage and counter espionage operations directed against Axis agents in Latin America. And on the more personal side, after Douglas suffered a near fatal horseback riding accident in 1949, Hoover sent Douglas a get-well message, joining Douglas's "host of friends" and "wishing [him] a speedy and complete recovery." Hoover closed by saying, "If there is anything I can do, please let me know." There were things to do, and while Douglas was recovering, the Bureau assisted him with his personal affairs. Plans were made for Justice Douglas to go hunting with two FBI special agents in the Arizona mountains after he recuperated from his injuries.

By the early 1950s, some high-level FBI officials began to question Justice Douglas's patriotism because of his Supreme Court decisions. Although Douglas had an open mind when it came to the political philosophy of others, there's no doubt that he was a liberal who had no love for the ideology of communism. Douglas was a strong anti-communist, and his sentiments varied little with Hoover's. And in a 1945 speech cited in a House Committee on Unamerican Activities report on the Communist Party USA, Douglas stated that "communism places state power in the hands of a small clique, who enforces that power by secret police with the weapons of murder and terror and sees to it that the people are deprived of the means of replacement and change." In 1948 Douglas gave a speech at the University of Florida, where he denounced communism as a force that planned world domination.

In 1955 Justice Douglas had relied upon the FBI to choose a "trustworthy" interpreter from a list of applicants he provided for his trip to Russia with Robert Kennedy. FBI Assistant Director Louis B. Nichols saw this as an opportunity to explain to Douglas, by then a critic of the government's loyalty programs, the FBI's internal security concerns. Nichols also said that the FBI had a moral and legal responsibility to stop a Supreme Court Justice from getting "mixed up with the wrong type of people if this can be avoided." To accomplish this lesson, two applicants with communist connections were used to demonstrate the use of confidential sources of information and exposing subversives, so that the value of informants could be forcefully brought to Justice Douglas's attention." Confidential sources were identified for Douglas, who was also given the information that they provided about the two applicants. According to the Bureau's sources, the two applicants were said to be members of the International Workers Order organization, subscribers to the *Daily Worker*, and contributors to the Joint Anti-Fascist Refugee Committee, among other associations that the Bureau considered suspect or outright subversive. The names of both applicants were also found in the FBI's security index, which listed persons believed to be potentially dangerous to internal security. Douglas did not choose either of these applicants, but it is not clear that his decision was influenced by the FBI's presentation.

It was about this time that the formally close relations between the Bureau and Douglas became an embarrassment to Hoover, who sought to keep it secret. Hoover's assistant, D.M. Ladd, noted several instances where "Justice Douglas rendered dissenting opinions, indicating his stand favorable to communist supported issues." When the Justice Department requested information about Douglas in 1954, a notation on the FBI documents made clear that even the attorney general was not to learn of the close relations. "Information not being disseminated: Cordial relations have existed between Justice Douglas and the Bureau since 1937."

The FBI files on Justice Douglas grew for another 12 years as agents collected hundreds of pages of information about Douglas' political views, his friends, and his sexual peccadillos. Justice

Douglas' court rulings ended his cordial relations with the FBI and its director.

MR. CHIEF JUSTICE EARL WARREN

Earl Warren, another former supporter of Hoover, had traded information and favors with the FBI before he arrived at the court. In 1933, when Warren was District Attorney, he set up the Anti-Racket Council of Alameda County, California. He enlisted Hoover's help. An agent was placed on the council's board of directors. Warren's office maintained its own files on subversive activities and offered them to the FBI. By 1937 Tolson had noted that Warren was quite "friendly" with the Bureau, friendly enough that an FBI car and chauffeur were offered to him during his stay in Washington. Warren wrote to Hoover to thank him for the courtesy shown him and to praise the FBI. "I still marvel at the progress you have made in the development of your great Bureau." Agents kept Hoover apprised of Warren's bright political future and his bid for the post of attorney general, a steppingstone to the governorship of California. The Warren-Hoover alliance burgeoned during Warren's tenure as attorney general and reached its peak during his governorship of California, with the development of a secret Bureau program entitled "Cooperation with Governor Earl Warren" that provided Warren with information from its files. From 1948 to 1953 Hoover authorized agents to furnish confidential information from the Bureau's files directly to Warren. For example, Hoover instructed agents in charge of the FBI office in San Francisco: "Advise governor Warren that the information is furnished in strictest confidence, and none of the information can be attributed to the FBI." Warren was not the only beneficiary. A nationwide FBI "Responsibilities Program" began in 1951 to provide information "regarding subjects of security index cards to a large number of state and local officials," such as friendly governors and other anti-communist government officials.

Requests for information made by Governor Warren illustrate the methods he used to combat the subversive threat during the

Cold War years, tactics that are inconsistent with his judicial legacy as the champion of civil liberties. Warren requested FBI information about his political opponents, labor union members, and state university employees, using the FBI program primarily to check for derogatory information about prospective political appointees or employees. Subversive references about a subject invariably led to dismissal or non-appointment. Warren often asked for FBI recommendations on whom he should appoint to state boards, including the state Crime Commission and the Athletic Commission. FBI officials were impressed that Warren never betrayed the Bureau as the source of information. Early in his career Warren may have benefited at the polls due to the FBI surveillance and disruption of leftist and Communist Party groups that were actively opposing him.

Governor Warren was a fervent advocate of law- and-order policies. He supported the internment of the Japanese during World War Two. He also was a committed anti-communist. He had grown up poor and was a liberal on social issues, such as state-funded medical insurance.

Despite his progressive streak, which set Warren apart from many other Republicans, President Eisenhower believed Warren was a solid moderate, who would offer no surprises while on the court. Eisenhower could not have been more wrong, and neither could Hoover.

By 1966 the tall, white-haired man had been Chief Justice for 12 years, and the FBI favors had stopped. In 1964 Warren had been removed from Hoover's "Special Correspondents List." The relationship had soured because of Warren Court rulings and the Warren Commission report concerning the assassination of John F. Kennedy. The report was mildly critical of the FBI.

MR. JUSTICE TOM CLARK

From all appearances, Hoover's best candidate to influence the Court in the Black case was the sixty-seven-year-old Tom C. Clark. The FBI director had more than a good friend in the former attorney general who favored bow ties and hailed from the Lone Star State. In 1948 Hoover had helped Clark's Supreme Court confirmation battle by providing him with ammunition about his opponents. Clark and the director saw eye-to-eye on law enforcement issues, and the justice had sought Hoover's off-the-record help on at least one opinion he had written.

On June 16, 1958, Justice Clark was working on his dissent in *Kent v. Dulles*, in which the authority of the secretary of state to ban the issuance of passports to American Communists was at issue. Clark phoned Hoover and said that he could not find anything in Hoover's book *Masters of Deceit* "concerning passport control." Clark asked, "if he could get a [public] statement . . . [by Hoover] . . . regarding the use of passports, particularly in the communist setup and their activities." Clark said he needed "a short paragraph, of three or four sentences, to attribute these remarks to some specific statement ... [by Hoover]." The director replied that he would be glad to help. Four days later, Hoover sent a letter by special messenger to Justice Clark at his chambers. The letter directed Clark to a passage in *Masters of Deceit* concerning Communist assistance to Soviet espionage agents, including the provision of false passports.

On June 16, 1958, Justice Douglas, writing for the 5-4 majority in *Kent v. Dulles*[46], struck down the secretary of state's passport policy. Justice Clark wrote for the dissent and cited Hoover, as he had on numerous other occasions, this time referring to *Masters of Deceit*

"[f]or a comprehensive story of Communism in America indicating the necessity for passport control."

There was no doubt that Clark revered Hoover. Justice Clark was not content to let his pro-government rulings speak for themselves. He reaffirmed his anti-radical and pro-law-and-order credentials in his steady correspondence with Hoover. Clark even aided the FBI's public relations and propaganda programs by working directly with Hoover to educate other judges about the Bureau's position on criminal law and national security matters.

And Clark kept Hoover apprised of how best to stay in the good graces of the largest organization of attorneys, the American Bar Association. One of Clark's law clerks in the early 1960s made his own contact with the Bureau at about the same time he received his job offer to work at the Court. The Bureau was eager to develop friends among Court employees.

Hoover rewarded Justice Clark by putting him on his "Special Correspondents List." Of course, Clark's opinions favoring the FBI and law enforcement in general were noted by the Bureau. In his letters, Clark praised Hoover's public critiques of the justice system and wrote to Hoover with some of his own criticism about the "foggy" area of search-and-seizure law that the Supreme Court had created. In 1966 Clark was still friendly with FBI agents, and he continued to receive personal favors from them.

The greatest apparent benefit to the FBI in approaching Justice Clark about the Black case was Clark's son, Ramsey, deputy attorney general in the Justice Department, was a friend of Cartha DeLoach. The younger Clark became Attorney General Nicholas Katzenbach's liaison to the FBI about the Black case.

Another asset for the FBI in approaching Clark was that he was "totally devoted" to President Johnson. In 1943, then Congressman Johnson had interceded with the Roosevelt administration to have Clark appointed an assistant attorney general. Almost twenty years later, on Tom Clark's request, Johnson helped Ramsey Clark get his first job at the Justice Department during the Kennedy administration. The elder Clark was a member of LBJ's dominos club – an informal group that included the president's friends, Justice Abe Fortas, Jack Brooks, Bill Deason, and Congressman J.J. Pickle – all of whom played dominos occasionally on Saturday afternoons when the president was ill.

And Johnson sometimes sought Justice Clark's advice. So, the Clarks, father and son, were friendly and beholden to President Johnson, who would benefit from Robert Kennedy being held responsible for the Black bugging. Though Justice Clark was the perfect candidate for Hoover to approach, Clark claimed that he never talked to Johnson or any other president about a pending case. And while Tom Clark had on at least one occasion been too free with information to a friend about the outcome of an upcoming ruling, his son, Ramsey, said that the justice had never talked to him about court cases.

MR. JUSTICE POTTER STEWART

Potter Stewart, another "get-tough-on-crime" justice, respected the FBI, even though Hoover turned him down for a job at the Bureau after Stewart graduated from Yale Law School. Stewart's wealthy Republican mother was in a group that opposed U.S. entry into World War II prior to Pearl Harbor. That was enough to keep the young Stewart from carrying an FBI badge. Hoover changed his opinion after Judge Stewart had proven himself on the federal appellate bench – to Hoover's liking. The director liked what he saw so well that Hoover helped Stewart get nominated for the Supreme Court.

But since Stewart did not know that Hoover had recommended him to the attorney general before his nomination, his support would not have seemed sure, and, even if Stewart had known, there was no reason to believe he would have violated his judicial oath.

MR. JUSTICE JOHN M. HARLAN

Former Wall Street lawyer and law enforcement advocate, Justice John M. Harlan was not likely to speak to the FBI about court business. President Eisenhower had nominated him on November 8, 1954, to fill the vacancy left by the death of Justice Robert Jackson. A lifelong Republican, Harlan had been chief counsel from 1951 to 1953 for the New York State Crime Commission, which investigated the relationship between organized crime and state government. His nomination had the hearty support of the American Bar Association committee on the Judiciary and the recommendation of the president's advisors, Thomas Dewey and Herbert Brownell.

The FBI had provided minor favors to Harlan over the years. When Hoover courted the powerful, he expected favors in return. But not even the director expected that a few small gratuities were enough to make Harlan receptive to judicial misconduct.

MR. JUSTICE BYRON WHITE

Justice Byron "Whizzer" White had been the "Paul Hornung of his day, a slashing, driving football halfback of matchless skills." Whizzer played professional football to pay his way through Yale law school as a Rhodes scholar. White became the law-and-order Kennedy appointee to the court. Since he had served directly under Attorney General Kennedy and was a colleague of Katzenbach, White was considered a Hoover enemy on the Black case because of his perceived pro-Kennedy bias. But Hoover thought he could dig up something to force White off the case: there were FBI memos sent to then Deputy Attorney General White about eavesdropping that would force him to disqualify himself.

MR. JUSTICE ABE FORTAS

Hoover knew that Fortas, Memphis born, and Yale Law School educated, was President Johnson's longtime friend and most trusted advisor. Johnson had, in fact, introduced Fortas to DeLoach, the FBI liaison to the White House. In large part, Johnson owed his 1948 senate election of Fortas's legal efforts, which ensured that his name was placed on the general election ballot after his contested victory in the runoff. The rough talking, arm twisting Texan usually got what he wanted, and succeeded alternately enticing and pressuring Kennedy appointee Arthur Goldberg off the court in 1965 to make way for Fortas, who required similar cajoling to accept the nomination to the so-called Jewish seat on the Court.

Concerned that Fortas might be attacked for political reasons, Johnson had asked the FBI to discover any opposition to Fortas' nomination to the court. On July 18, 1965, President Johnson phoned DeLoach and told him that he was thinking about appointing Fortas to an "important departmental position."

Johnson wanted the FBI to find out "what opposition he would encounter after he named Fortas" to this unspecified position. Johnson told DeLoach to have agents interview Senators Eugene McCarthy and Robert and Edward Kennedy as well as some conservative senators to get them on record so they could not later issue negative press statements. Johnson told DeLoach he did not care that Fortas belonged to "communist front organizations" in the early 1940s. Fortas "had matured" and was now well trusted and loyal. And what might be an understatement, Johnson said "he trusted Fortas as much as he did Lady Bird."

DeLoach, a southerner like Johnson and Fortas, was the perfect man for the president's job, he was as close to Johnson as Fortas was. Johnson had even installed the direct line to the White House into DeLoach's bedroom. Not even Hoover was so privileged. By the mid-1960s, Johnson was not entirely trusting of the cranky septuagenarian Hoover, and he bypassed the director in favor of DeLoach. DeLoach, was the administration's informant in the American Legion while serving as the head of the FBI crime records division, which often acted as the Bureau's publicity and propaganda section. He was responsible for publicizing the Bureau's achievements, mobilizing friends in the media to attack FBI enemies, and keeping the issue of crime and the communist menace in the public eye.

After Johnson introduced Fortas to DeLoach the two men were soon working together on very sensitive matters at Johnson's behest. During the U.S. intervention in the civil war in the Dominican Republic in 1965, Fortas called Hoover and DeLoach to convey the president's orders about Bureau actions.

DeLoach's interviews with eleven senators turned up no opposition to Fortas. President Johnson asked the FBI to do a rush background investigation. The investigation covered all the usual subjects: character, loyalty, reputation, and legal ability. There was no investigation of Fortas's sources of income. Other than a laundry list of subversive references and classified reports about Fortas' advice to the president on foreign policy matters, the investigation was unremarkable.

On July 28, 1965, Johnson nominated Fortas to the Supreme Court. Fortas said he initially rejected the offer to nominate him to the court, writing, "I want a few more years to try to be of service to you and the Johnson family... and to stabilize the law firm ." But under pressure from the president, Fortas accepted the appointment. He wrote to Johnson pleading that he did not want his presence on the court to change their relationship: "I can only hope that you will continue to see me and to call upon me for anything that I can do to help." Johnson was happy to oblige.

At his Senate confirmation hearing, Fortas under oath denied that his friendship with Johnson would interfere with his work on the court. He also countered the time worn charges that he agreed with communists in addition to representing them. Even Senate Judiciary Committee chairman, Dixiecrat James O. Eastland, who was also the head of the Senate Internal Security committee, took no interest in the allegations about Fortas' ties to communists. After twenty minutes of debate on the floor of the senate, Fortas was confirmed as an associate justice on August 11, 1965. The Senate, the same day, confirmed Thurgood Marshall as its first Black solicitor general of the United States.

After Fortas moved into the Supreme Court building, it was not long before he called his "boss" to give the president the number of the private line into his chambers. The other justices were aware of this direct line to the White House, and it made some of them uncomfortable. Nevertheless, Fortas continued to have regular telephone contact with the president and frequent written correspondence. While Fortas sat on the Supreme Court, he continued to act as the president's informal legal counsel. He suggested judicial appointments, passed on legislation, and attended White House meetings. Fortas continued to advise Johnson about everything from the Vietnam War policy to urban riots.

In January 1966 Jack Valenti, Johnson's special assistant, sent a light-hearted letter to Justice Fortas praising a recent speech Fortas had made. "If you keep up with this speech making, I'm going to suggest to the president that we get in the Supreme

Court business - you're poaching on our preserve."[47] Joking or not, Valenti was right. Fortas was acting like a presidential adviser, not a justice of the Supreme Court. And soon the White House and the FBI would be getting into the Supreme Court business. The separation of powers square dance that Hoover had choreographed was about to begin. The executive branch would be leading, swinging its judicial partner.[48]

CHAPTER 7: FADE TO BLACK

When the Supreme Court denied *cert* in the Black case, both justices Fortas and White participated in the court's decision to let the conviction stand. After the solicitor general's May 24th disclosure that federal agents had eavesdropped on Black and his lawyer, Fortas formally disqualified himself from participation in the case. He sent a short note to Chief Justice Warren on June 10, before the conference was held that same day. White also disqualified himself, but not until Saturday, June 11, the day after the conference. In a letter to the chief justice, White explained that Marshall had personally advised him that a May 1961 memo from Hoover to White when he was deputy attorney general had been brought to his attention. Hoover had sent copies of the memo to Katzenbach and to Marshall on June 3, to prove that Robert Kennedy had approved the bugging. The 1961 memo to White said that "in the interests of national security, microphone surveillance is also utilized by the FBI on a restricted basis, even though trespass is necessary, in uncovering major criminal activities." Trespass was a euphemism for saying that the bug was illegally installed, either after a burglary or after a hole was drilled through the wall.

To make sure the White House knew the "truth," Hoover also sent a copy of his memo to Johnson special assistant Marvin Watson, and he continued to keep Watson up to date about his battle with the attorney general over Black v. U.S. On the morning of June 7, DeLoach and Ramsey Clark met in Watson's office at the White House.

Marshall probably had good intentions when he notified White of the FBI memo, however this contact made in the absence of Black's lawyers was an *ex parte* contact as lawyers refer to it which gives the appearance of favoritism and unfair advantage. It is an ethical violation for an attorney involved in litigation to contact the judge or justice about the merits of the case without his opponent's knowledge. Yet the Justice Department made it a policy to contact Justice White when they "ran across his tracks" in a case.

At the June 1 conference the court had already discussed the Black case. By the Friday, June 10, conference, the decision to issue the order in Black had already been discussed and voted upon. The justices decided that Warren would prepare an order requiring the government to provide the details about the surveillance of Black. Warren's proposed order noted at the bottom that "Mr. Justice Fortas took no part in the consideration or decision of this order."

Despite Justice White's participation at the conference, White in his June 11 letter, asked Warren to add an addendum to the Black order before it was issued that Monday. "In view of these matters about the Hoover memo to me concerning the FBI's use of bugging," White wrote, "the upcoming order should indicate "that I took no part in the issuance of the order." White had taken part in the issuance of the order the day before. Hoover had won a substantial victory: a likely pro-Kennedy vote would not be forthcoming.

On June 13, the High Court directed a most unusual order to the government in the Black case:

> The court desires a response from the government in this case, not limited to, but directed in particular toward the kind of apparatus used by the government; the person or persons who authorized its installation; the statute or Executive Order relied upon; the date or dates of installation; whether there is an existence of recording of the conversations heard; when the information concerning petitioner came into the hands of any attorney for the government and into which ones, as well as what use was made of the

information in the case against petitioner.[49]

Chief Justice Warren followed White's instruction. "Mr. Justice White and Mr. Justice Fortas took no part in the consideration or decision of this order."

That same day Hoover had DeLoach phone Justice Fortas privately to provide the "true facts."[50]

Fortas returned DeLoach's call late the same night. DeLoach said that he wanted to see him about the Black case in confidence that that he recognized Fortas might view this as a "violation of judicial ethics."[51] Fortas said that he would meet with DeLoach about the Black case or "any other matter in confidence." The two men agreed to meet at Fortas' home the next morning. Looking back twenty-four years later, DeLoach said his "primary purpose in seeking out Justice Fortas was to prevent former attorney general Kennedy from causing Fortas to believe that the FBI had acted without authority in the Black case."[52]

DeLoach, who had studied law at Stetson university, and Hoover, who had a bachelor's and a master's degree of law from George Washington University, knew it was grossly improper to approach a justice about a pending case, especially a case in which he was involved. DeLoach was described by a Washington reporter as a "rattlesnake" and Hoover's "hatchet man." He was very good at his job. The meeting with Fortas was one of DeLoach's most important missions.

At breakfast DeLoach talked to Fortas about the Black case. He said that Attorney General Katzenbach planned to present a "slanted version" to the Supreme Court" in an effort to protect Kennedy who, DeLoach maintained, had authorized the installation of the bugs in Black's hotel suite. It was a fight for the presidency, Fortas chimed in: "LBJ versus Kennedy. Senator Kennedy was trying to capture Vice President Hubert Humphry's liberals. If Kennedy's approval of this bugging were made public," Fortas said, "Kennedy would be completely destroyed."[53] Johnson and Fortas shared their hatred for Robert Kennedy, and John Kennedy was no better, as far as Johnson and Hoover were concerned. President Kennedy had reportedly said that the three most overrated things in the world were "the state of Texas, the FBI and the political wizardry of LBJ."

Fortas told DeLoach that the "dumb" solicitor general had "ineptly and inadequately" presented the matter of the bugging to the court. Fortas said that although he and Justice White had disqualified themselves, they both attended the conference meeting and discussed the case. The other justices, except for White, who had worked in the Justice Department with Kennedy and Katzenbach, believed that the court needed to order the government to provide it with information about this bugging to prevent Katzenbach from handpicking a federal District Court judge favorable to Kennedy who might blast the FBI. Douglas and Black were especially eager to get more information about who had authorized the eavesdropping. Fortas told the DeLoach that the Supreme Court had only two options: they could send the case back to the District Court or could completely overturn the conviction. Fortas believed the court would send the case back to the District Court for another trial.

DeLoach gave Fortas seven memos about specific microphone surveillances, including one memo Kennedy signed. There were no memos from Kennedy granting Hoover general authority to employ non-national security microphone surveillances after trespassing on the target's property. But orally and in writing, Kennedy had been put on notice that the FBI had illegally installed bugs in organized crime cases. Fortas agreed with DeLoach that Katzenbach would slant his reply to the questions posed by the court. The best thing for Fortas to do was "slip in the back door and see the president" at the White House and tell him what was going on.

Fortas and DeLoach also discussed the possibility of setting up a confidential arbiter to compose the government's response to the court, to take the decision out of Katzenbach's hands. Fortas suggested Kenneth Royall, former secretary of the army or Lewis Powell, former president of the American Bar Association, to head up the Commission. DeLoach said that Powell had generally supported Hoover's view on criminal matters, but on occasion he had been "somewhat naive and a little weak."

Fortas said that he had already taken steps to disqualify himself in the Jimmy Hoffa case and wanted to know if Kennedy also had been involved in any irregularities regarding that case. DeLoach said that Kennedy was behind a bug on one of Hoffa's attorneys - a man named James Haggerty. DeLoach claimed that the microphone was installed, even though the Bureau was against it. Fortas said that he would sit with the rest of the supreme court on the Hoffa case and that he would "make certain that Kennedy was exposed." He believed that the supreme court would affirm the decision of the lower court in the Hoffa case based on his conversations with the other justices.

At the meeting Fortas also reminded DeLoach that he had secured the favorable reference to the FBI in the *Miranda v. Arizona*[54] decision, a ruling written by Chief Justice Warren, that had been handed down the day before. The case that established the Miranda warnings the right to hire counsel and the right to remain silent that police officers must read to criminal defendants prior to custodial interrogations. Fortas before oral arguments had advised other members of the court that the "Federal Bureau of Investigation had for many years advised subjects of their rights." As a result of Fortas's *ex parte* conversation with the DeLoach, the *Miranda* decision praised the FBI for its policy of reading suspects their rights prior to interrogating them.

At the breakfast meeting with Fortas, DeLoach said that Johnson supported the FBI's use of eavesdropping in the security and criminal fields, but not for political purposes. Fortas said he knew that the FBI was not guilty of such things but that it was Kennedy's practices that led to the "hysteria" about wiretapping and bugging currently underway. Fortas said he would call the president.

Fortas phoned Johnson before catching a mid-morning flight to Florida to meet with his benefactor, financier Louis Wolfson. DeLoach left Fortas's home to brief Hoover. The director was amazed that Fortas had not "weaseled out" by refusing to meet with DeLoach about a pending court case. The director had doubts about setting up a pro-Johnson arbiter to investigate the authorization of the Black bug because it might turn into another "Warren Commission and end up in a fiasco." The Black case was the "greatest crisis" the FBI had ever faced, Hoover said. "We have got to fight to save our lives." DeLoach agreed.

Hoover told DeLoach that Fortas was not the only justice to secretly speak to the government about a case. According to Hoover a Justice Department official "went to see two justices of the Supreme Court... about the Giancana case in Chicago and he was advised that if it came before the Supreme Court, it would be reversed." Hoover said that the Justice Department dropped the case as a result of this conversation.[55] "Giancana" was apparently Sam Giancana, the Chicago mobster whom the CIA allegedly recruited to assassinate Fidel Castro in 1960 and who reportedly had a mistress in common with President Kennedy.

On Tuesday, June 21, Fortas called DeLoach to tell him that the president had decided to set up a three-person, pro-Johnson Commission on electronic surveillance, not a single arbiter. That afternoon Fortas spent two and a half hours with the president at the White House, the last hour in the presidential living quarters on the second floor. DeLoach also dropped in at the White House that afternoon to visit Marvin Watson. DeLoach called LBJ from Watson's office. LBJ was in the presidential living quarters to discuss the press release that Fortas had ghost written about the creation of the wiretapping Commission. The president put forward this suggestion when on the phone and the justice agreed to remove language in the press release to which DeLoach objected. Fortas had collected so many documents from the FBI and the White House about the Black case that he created two secret file folders apart from his official court records on the case.

Hoover employed many avenues to Johnson. Even before DeLoach saw Watson on June 21, Hoover had already spoken on the phone that day with Watson about the Black case. Hoover reiterated his view Katzenbach was trying to protect Kennedy from the fallout of authorizing illegal surveillances. At the end of the day Watson briefed the president about his talks with DeLoach and Hoover.

The next day, Wednesday, June 22, Attorney General Katzenbach held an afternoon staff meeting at his office about the Black case that was attended by Ramsey Clark, among others. On Thursday, Fortas and Johnson decided to scrap the wiretapping commission. That afternoon Fortas called Watson who had spoken with DeLoach that morning. Less than ten minutes after Fortas got off the phone with Watson, Ramsey Clark also called Watson.

While DeLoach had Fortas working within the court and with the president, DeLoach himself was working with Ramsey Clark to change the wording of the Justice Department supplemental memorandum, the government's response to the court's questions about who had authorized the bugging and under what legal authority. Except in written communications, Hoover never tried to discuss the Black case directly with Katzenbach, though DeLoach did. According to Katzenbach, even when he met with Hoover and the president in the Oval Office on Saturday morning, June 25 to discuss FBI agents in the Dominican Republic, the Black case was not mentioned. And Katzenbach never discussed the Black case with the president at cabinet meetings or elsewhere, believing it was better for Johnson not to be involved in the case. The attorney general had no idea that Hoover was going directly to the White House, attempting to influence the government's response behind his back.

On June 28 DeLoach met with Ramsey Clark to raise objections to the department's proposed supplemental memorandum. That memo, to be issued by the solicitor general's office, had to be approved by Katzenbach. As proposed, the memo was going to say that "the director of the FBI authorized the listening device" or "permission to place a listening device was given by a duly constituted authority." The FBI objected to either formulation. DeLoach told Clark it was because Robert Kennedy had authorized the bugging. DeLoach said that he did not want to "request an audience before the Supreme Court" or to "put the absolute truth in a formal press release," but he would do that if he was forced. This was another in the line of threats. Earlier the Bureau had warned Ramsey Clark that if the supplemental memo was not the "truth," the FBI was "perfectly willing to lay the evidence before Senator Long's Committee." Long had already communicated to the Justice Department that he was willing to hold hearings on the Black case. Clark passed on DeLoach's warning to Katzenbach.

While the battle over the wording of the supplemental memorandum continued, DeLoach kept working on Watson, repeating the admonition that the attorney general was a Kennedy man and not to be trusted. On July 11 DeLoach asked Watson to remind Ramsey Clark that Johnson supported Hoover's position that Kennedy had authorized the bugging. DeLoach said that Ramsey Clark had evidently forgotten the earlier talk they had had at the White House. Watson equivocated; he and the president were in a precarious position on the Black case because they did not want to be seen as undermining their attorney general. Watson said that he would have a talk with Ramsey Clark if the opportunity presented itself.

That same day Ramsey Clark called Justice Brennan's chambers. Brennan's law clerk returned the call. His message was recorded as: "we'll be glad to help you if he can or will have Justice Brennan call you himself when he returns." On July 11 and 12, before the Justice Department filed its brief in the Black case, Justice Brennan and Ramsey Clark apparently spoke on the phone. Ramsey Clark's telephone logs at the Johnson library do not reflect the content of this conversation.

On July 13, despite the machinations of Hoover, Watson, and Fortas, Katzenbach's position on the Black case prevailed. The Justice Department's supplemental memorandum to the Supreme Court blamed Hoover for the bugging.

> No specific statute or executive order was relied upon in the installation of the listening device in question.... Attorneys General have delegated to the director of the Federal Bureau of Investigation the duty to gather intelligence to investigate violation of

federal laws, and to collect evidence in cases in which the United States is or may be a party.... Under Departmental practice in effect for a period of years prior to 1963, and continuing into 1965, the Director of the Federal Bureau of Investigation was given authority to approve the installation of devices such as that in question for intelligence (and not evidentiary) purposes when required in the interest of internal security or national safety, including organized crime, kidnappings and matters wherein human life might be at stake. Acting on the basis of the aforementioned Departmental of authorization, the Director approved installation of the device involved in the instant case.

The government's supplemental memorandum stated that Hoover had been granted broad authority to conduct microphone surveillance. In addition to the threat of an FBI press release or a Congressional investigation, Hoover's agents had enlisted the help of the last Republican attorney general, William Rogers, to support the director's contention that he had been granted general authority to bug in organized crime cases, despite the fact that this arguable grant of authority was not committed to paper by Rogers. Every attorney general, including Kennedy, had used information the FBI provided, and they did not want to know how it was obtained.

The Justice Department memo in the Black case confirmed what many had suspected about FBI eavesdropping. *Newsweek* reported that the FBI was "effectively exposed by its parent agency, the Justice Department, as an opportunistic and occasionally illegal user of eavesdropping devices." The disclosure July 13, 1966, may be "the most embarrassing day of the FBI's fifty-year life .... faced with this awkward revelation, the Bureau officially held to its time-honored *modus operandi* - never apologize, never explain." The magazine said the "most startling admission" was that until 1965 "the FBI had standing authority to install eavesdropping devices in the homes and offices of any American citizen" when it decided internal security or the fight against organized crime required it.

Hoover had nobody to blame but himself for the Black fiasco. He was finally caught exploiting the see no evil, hear no evil policies of his bosses. Hoover's only shred of hope to avoid being singled out by the Supreme Court as the one who authorized the Fourth Amendment violation and being forced out of his job a year after Johnson had exempted him from retirement at age of seventy, rested with Justice Fortas or with Justice Clark.

But Hoover was not going to wait for the Supreme Court to act. Katzenbach had stood his ground with Hoover, and an attorney general who is not an FBI patsy threatened all unauthorized or extra-legal Bureau activities. As a result, Hoover started to change Bureau practices. Less than a week after the government filed its response in Black, a memo was circulated among ranking officials at FBI headquarters. "We do not obtain authorization for "black bag" jobs from outside the Bureau. Such a technique involves trespassing and is clearly illegal; Therefore, it would be impossible to obtain any legal sanction for it. Despite this, 'black bag' [burglaries] jobs have been used because they represent an invaluable technique in combating subversive activities of a clandestine nature aimed directly at undermining and destroying our nation."

The memo further said that assistant director Clyde Tolson or Hoover himself had to approve each burglary and that the authorization was not to be filed with regular FBI records. Despite the implication that "black bag" jobs were to continue, a note at the end of the memo stated that these "surreptitious entries" would no longer be approved. Old Bureau hands knew that if such jobs were going to be approved in the future, authorization would be given orally.

Although Justices Fortas and Byron White had formally disqualified themselves from participating in the Black case both men continued to receive copies of proposed opinions circulated by the other justices. Fortas and White did not vote in Black, but they were present in the conference room when the case was debated, and Fortas continued to lobby informally and covertly.

The memos that Hoover sent to Watson had been passed to

Fortas. Justice Fortas would place them in a secret file about the Black case. In fact, Justice Fortas maintained four files on the Black case – two official court files and two secret files. The first file was the official Black court folder, which contained copies of the opinions and memos circulated by the other justices. Other internal court documents related to Black were filed in the Davis case folder, in the eavesdropping case that would be decided that same time by the court. This folder was Fortas's second official file about case matters related to the Black case. The third Black folder was the secret file on the case. It contained FBI documents given to Fortas by Watson, some of which contained the original White House stamp recording the date and time at which they were received. In addition to five FBI memos, this file contained a blind memo, unsigned and undated, simply entitled "BLACK." The fourth file was entitled "Technical and Microphone Surveillances." This file contained FBI documents that DeLoach gave Fortas at their June 14 breakfast meeting. This included the 1961 Hoover to White memo and a memo showing that Robert Kennedy had signed an authorization for a leased telephone microphone setup in New York City that same year.[56]

The two-page blind memo entitled "BLACK" stated: "1) Where the government admits that, by means of a microphone installed through the wall of petitioner's hotel suite, it has monitored conversations between petitioner and his counsel, have petitioner's constitutional rights been violated regardless of the use or non-use of the fruits of the monitoring? 2) Did it make any difference that the tape recordings of the bug had been erased? 3) When and how were Justice Department officials 'made aware of the installation of the listening device?'"

The last question echoed one of Hoover's ongoing concerns in his battle with Katzenbach over the wording of the government's memoranda sent to the court. Hoover had written an angry letter to Katzenbach on May 26, pointing out that the solicitor general's first memorandum to the court, which said "long after the trial, in the fall of 1965, attorneys in the criminal division of the DOJ learned that a listening device had been installed in

Black's suite" was false. Hoover reminded Katzenbach that he had personally sent him a memo on August 24, 1965, advising that the microphone used against Black had picked up conversations with Bobby Baker, but not mentioning that Black's lawyer had been picked up as well. The FBI had argued that the attorney general should have disclosed details of the bugging to the D.C. Court of Appeals as soon as he learned of them, before the Circuit Court of Appeals affirmed the conviction on November 10, 1965, and before the Supreme Court decided to consider the case.

Due to Hoover's prompting, the government's supplemental memorandum to the court correctly stated that the FBI had initially told the Justice Department about the bugging of Black in August 1965, more than a year after Black's conviction for tax evasion. Justice Fortas suggested that the solicitor general be asked when the Justice Department first learned about the bugging, which would spread some of the blame to the Justice Department for withholding information. This third question had been raised after four days of receiving copies of the FBI memos from Watson and DeLoach claiming that the Justice Department was not being truthful in its proposed response to the court.

Justice Fortas framed the issues about the FBI's notification of the Justice Department in such a way as to divert attention away from the FBI by calling into question the Justice Department's assertions about when it learned of the interceptions. It is not clear how Fortas circulated this memo because, unlike the official correspondence between the justices clearly signaling the chambers from which it was issued and the date of issuance, Fortas's memo had neither a name nor a date. But the memo was circulated. One copy is in John Harlan's papers, stapled to a draft of Harlan's dissent in the case. Not only had Fortas reported the justices' conference discussions to the White House and to the FBI, but he also worked to influence the conference debate. This was the biggest breach of legal ethics by a justice in the history of the Supreme Court.

Chief Justice Warren assigned the job of writing the Black

opinion to Hoover's longtime ally Tom Clark. Clark was also to write the opinion concerning the Davis case, which dealt with the related eavesdropping issue. A federal prisoner, Davis, had been held temporarily in a Florida state jail, where jailers had installed tape recorders in the walls of the cells in which the prisoners met their visitors. Davis claimed that conversations with his attorney might have been taped. The court was divided over the issue of whether the court should require the solicitor general to provide information about whether Davis's conversations were recorded.

The Davis and Black cases had both been set for conference on October 3, but Justice Potter Stewart wanted more time to think about Davis, and the cases were rescheduled to October 14. At that conference, Clark, Douglas, Fortas, and Warren wanted the government to tell the court whether Davis' cell had been bugged. The rest of the justices wanted to have the District Court determine the issue by sending the case down for a new trial. Justice Black was adamant that it was "wholly and completely inappropriate" to make the government respond. "I can think of no possible circumstance under which a mere monitoring of the conversation between the defendant... and his lawyer would justify a dismissal of the case."

The Black case was even more problematic. Justice White had been indirectly implicated in that illegality, due to his receipt of the Hoover memo about microphones installed by trespass. In the average case accepted by the Supreme Court for review, oral argument is scheduled after both parties to a controversy have sent their legal briefs to the court. The opposing attorneys respectively argued their case and are interrogated by the nine justices in the courtroom. On the Friday after oral argument, at 10 a.m. the justices retired to the conference room to vote but the Black case was no ordinary case.

At a later conference discussion of the Black case, at least four of the justices had voted to hold the oral argument and ask the solicitor general a number of questions. It looked like the FBI source from September 12 who had predicted that the court would put Solicitor General Marshall on the "griddle" at oral argument was indeed "reliable." Justice Harlan strongly disapproved of the unprecedented procedure of asking factual questions to the government at oral argument. Had Fortas, during conference, convinced the rest of the court to interrogate Marshall during oral argument in attempt to "expose Kennedy's role in authorizing the bugging"?

Justice Harlan had not bought any of it: he wrote to his brethren:

> I wish to record my disagreement with the step taken today in the unusual situation that this case presents.... without anything more before than the representations made by both sides, the court has set Black's petition for reconsideration of the denial of *cert* for oral argument on three questions propounded in its order. I think this unusual procedure is precipitous, ill advised, and out of keeping with orderly judicial process.

Harlan believed that the facts of the case had yet to be determined. As such, he continued:

> [A]n inquiry should be conducted in the customary manner through adversary proceedings at the trial level and not by means of colloquy with the solicitor general in our courtroom. The orderly process is to remand this case to the District Court for a hearing and findings on the occurrences in question.

On October 20, Justice Clark circulated a memo to his brethren suggesting that Davis and Black be handled jointly because of the "close relationship of the single issue in each case." Clark proposed *cert* be denied to Davis, which would leave the bugging to be decided by the District Court. As for the Black case, Clark, despite his pro-Hoover bias, knew that Black's constitutional right to counsel has been violated by the FBI bug. Clark wrote: "The appearance of justice, like Caesar's wife, must be beyond reproach." Justice Black's absolutist position on the 4th Amendment was that the invasion of privacy issue itself was irrelevant because the 4th Amendment protects citizens against unreasonable searches and seizures of "persons, houses, and effects," not seizure of words. So, despite the intrusiveness of the bugging, Justice Black prevailed upon Clark to remove the references to the constitution, as this would "indicate that we are passing on the constitutionality now - I do not want to do that." Black also objected to the reference to Caesar's wife, for reasons that he did not articulate. On October 25 at 10:30 a.m., Fortas called DeLoach at FBI headquarters and "expressed appreciation for the information the director had passed along to him about a confidential matter." DeLoach responded that the FBI was "concerned about the Black case" and asked, "if he knew when the decision would be handed down." Fortas replied that there would be a decision on Monday, November 7th. DeLoach asked if the FBI "should prepare for the worst – a sweeping proclamation denouncing the use of electronic devices." Fortas said that "the court's thinking had changed concerning this matter since they last talked." According to Fortas, "the court actually felt that the Black case and its various problems should not be handled at the Supreme Court level." By this, DeLoach understood Fortas to be saying that "the Black case was to be remanded to the lower court." DeLoach reported his conversation to Hoover and Tolson. Hoover ordered DeLoach to "find out the identity of the judge who handled the matter in the lower court." Fortas' unethical contact with the FBI once again gave the Bureau a tactical advantage. They had a voluminous file called "Federal Judges" with background information on hundreds of judges.

At the next Supreme Court conference, Clark's proposal to handle Black and Davis together was accepted with minor revisions by Warren, Douglas, Black, and Brennan. Fortas and White had agreed to the joint handling of Davis and Black and both had participated in the Davis ruling. Douglas was so confused by White's and Fortas' participation in only part of the joint Davis and Black ruling that his conference notes show that White voted with the majority to vacate and remand the Black case to district court while Fortas did not participate in Black.

It was decided that the majority's joint opinion in Davis and Black would not be signed by Justice Clark, its primary author. An unsigned opinion, called a *per curiam* ruling, is often used for unimportant rulings - or in the most important decisions, when the court desires the appearance of speaking with one voice.

As Fortas advised the FBI, on November 7, the Supreme Court issued a two-and-a-half page *per curiam* decision vacating Black's conviction and sending the case back to the district court for a new trial. The FBI bugging of Black's suite picked up conversations between Black and his attorney. Justices Harlan and Stewart dissented, believing that the case should first be sent back to the trial court to resolve the issue about whether a new trial was necessary since the government claimed it did not use any information from the microphone surveillance in his tax case. The ruling did not mention Hoover. Once again, the FBI director's illegal conduct, while embarrassing, did not affect his position. Hoover was fortunate: he had Justice Fortas as an informer and public relations man and old friend Justice Clark writing the opinion in Black. The director was also skillful enough to let the chief justice and Fortas know that Justice White, the second in command at the Justice Department the year before the Black bugging, received at least one FBI memo about Bureau eavesdropping practices.

The language of the Black opinion was clinical and without passion, offering no indication that the justices were outraged by the FBI's actions. The justices did not quote the words of Justice Felix Frankfurter in the 1954 *Irvine vs. California*[57] case involving bugging accomplished by trespass: "when any person is intentionally deprived of his constitutional rights those responsible have committed no ordinary offense. A crime of this nature, is subtly encouraged by failure to condemn and punish, certainly leads down the road to totalitarianism." Instead, the ruling ended with the assertion: "Mr. Justice White and Mr. Justice Fortas took no part in the consideration or decision of this case."

Black was subsequently acquitted at his retrial. In December 1966, the fight over who had authorized the illegal FBI ELSUR

– Hoover or Kennedy – was splashed over the front pages of the nation's newspapers. The Black case changed the way the Department of Justice informed the courts of electronic surveillance and required the FBI to set up an electronic surveillance (ELSUR) index of wiretaps and bugs. This index still excluded some illegal ELSUR such as those directed at Dr. Rev. Martin Luther King, Jr.

Despite the battle in the press and at the White House over electronic snooping, the Supreme Court in 1966 still had not ruled that warrantless wiretapping, accomplished without trespass, was a violation of the 4th Amendment.[58]

CHAPTER 8: THE FORTAS FILM FESTIVAL BIDS GOODBYE TO JUSTICE FORTAS

During the summer of 1968, the Warren Court had begun its painful last throes. Champion boxer Muhammad Ali's[59] 1964 admonition to the Reverend Martin Luther King – "watch out for them whities" - might have been sound advice for Abe Fortas. Fortas, like Ali, had been picked up in the electronic eavesdropping devices directed at King.[60] During the turbulent summer and fall of 1968, Fortas was Earl Warren's heir apparent as chief justice.

Newspapers carried headlines about political assassinations - King, then Robert Kennedy - inner cities aflame, Black Panthers, Students for a Democratic Society, anti-war demonstrators, hippies and yippies. America was preoccupied with issue of crime, which often coalesced with issues of the Vietnam War and race relations. Congressional action to fight crime culminated in the passage of the Omnibus Crime Control and Safe Streets Act of 1968. Title III of the Act regulated the interception of wire and oral communications. After obtaining a judicial warrant, the FBI was allowed to wiretap or bug to obtain evidence of specified crimes. Warrants could be authorized for electronic surveillance directed at serious Atomic Energy Act offenses as well as offenses relating to espionage, sabotage, treason, riot, murder, kidnapping, robbery, extortion, presidential assassination, and a host of other offenses. Electronic surveillance provisions were drawn to meet the constitutional requirements for electronic surveillances enunciated by the 1967 Supreme Court rulings in *Berger v. New York* and *Katz v. U.S.*[61] But a question still open was the constitutional power of the president to wiretap and bug without a warrant for "national security" reasons.

In *Katz* the FBI had installed a bug in a telephone booth without a warrant. Justice Fortas voted with the majority that this violated the Fourth Amendment. There was nothing in the FBI's files that showed Hoover, or his men had made on overture to Fortas on this case.

After being nominated for chief justice, Justice Abe Fortas testified before the Senate Judiciary Committee in 1968:

> I cannot conceive of any president of the United States, and certainly not this President, talking to a Supreme Court Justice, whether his own nominee or not, about anything that might possibly come before the court... Presidents of the United States do not do that: Justices of the Supreme Court would not tolerate it. That is our country, Senator [Ervin]. That is our country.

Neither the Johnson White House nor the FBI contradicted this false testimony. The Bureau was not asked to do a follow-up background investigation of Fortas. Attorney General Ramsey Clark, who apparently didn't know of Fortas' unethical dealing with Hoover, considered an FBI investigation of a sitting justice a separation of powers violation, a violation of the constitution. Fortas told Senators:

> [S]ince I have been a Justice, the President of the United States has never, directly or indirectly, approximately or remotely, talked to me about anything before the Court or that might come before the Court. I want to make that absolutely clear. [I have participated] in conferences on critical matters having nothing whatever to do with any legal situation or with anything before the Court.[62]

Fortas also lied about his role as presidential speech writer and drafter of legislation while on the Court.[63]

Senator Robert P. Griffin, a Republican opponent of Fortas' elevation, approached DeLoach on September 23, 1968, to dig up dirt on Fortas. DeLoach said that was "impossible" to help as the Attorney General would have to authorize it and he supported Fortas. Senator Strom Thurmond's office also contacted the FBI to confirm derogatory information on Fortas about his former representation of the publisher of a "girlie magazine." "It appears prudent that we not get involved in any such opposition [to Fortas]." Hoover scrawled, "Yes" at the bottom of the memo.[64]

DeLoach had invited Justice Fortas and his wife to a small dinner party at his home, along with Attorney General Clark and an assistant attorney general. On another occasion, DeLoach attended a chamber music concert at Fortas' home. DeLoach was being counted on by the White house to help out in the push to get Fortas confirmed as chief justice.[65]

DeLoach and Hoover could have destroyed Fortas' confirmation chances and given the Senate grounds for impeachment. But Fortas' secrets stayed buried in Hoover's office files.

Conservative opposition pounced on Fortas' receipt of $15,000 from wealthy benefactors for a series of lectures he had given during the summer of 1967 at American University. His rulings in obscenity, criminal, and subversive cases were described by a conservative senator as "appalling." A so-called Fortas Film Festival was held by Senator Strom Thurmond, a Dixiecrat turned Republican. Senators were treated to pornographic movies Thurmond claimed Fortas had found not obscene such as *Flaming Creatures*.[66] The movie was said to be a "campy costume melodrama" in which "garishly dressed men and women with exposed genitalia [engage] in a pantomime of sexual activity."

Within days of the Senate vote, Johnson withdrew the nomination. The Senate had no idea that Justice Fortas had been an FBI informant.

On November 5, 1968, Richard M. Nixon won the presidency. Soon there would be a new attorney general, John N. Mitchell.

Every Fortas ruling involving the FBI was tainted by his prior unethical behavior and the ever-present threat of blackmail. He should have recused himself in every matter involving the FBI or the Justice Department.

In 1969, Justice Fortas dissented in an overturned FBI prosecution of gambler William Spinelli,[67] finding the Bureau's search warrant insufficient under the Fourth Amendment. Justice Fortas disagreed writing that "A policeman's affidavit should not be judged as an entry in an essay contest. It is not 'abracadabra.'" His argument in *Spinelli* is interesting considering Justice Fortas' own history with an accusation he argued was false, made by an FBI informant. "Although Spinelli's reputation, standing alone would not, of course, justify the search, this Court has held that such a reputation may make the informer's report much less subject to skepticism than would be such a charge against one without such a history."[68]

In another 1969 case, Justice Fortas dissented in part, more like a presidential advisor or FBI advocate than criminal defense attorney or jurist. In *Alderman v. U.S.*,[69] a trio of electronic surveillance cases, which were so important to the Justice Department that an emissary was sent to the Supreme Court to privately, unethically, and unsuccessfully ask the justices to reverse their decision against the government.

Jack C. Landau, director of public information at the Justice Department, an acquaintance of Justice Brennan, first approached Brennan. Landau said that the president, attorney general, solicitor general, FBI, and CIA were very concerned that the government might have to dismiss many prosecutions in which criminal defendants were inadvertently overheard by ELSUR devices directed at the 125 foreign embassies in Washington, DC. The government didn't want this information to become public.

Brennan referred Landau to Chief Justice Warren who listened then told him that his overture was improper. The *ex parte* contact with the Court was not disclosed to the criminal defense attorneys. After Watergate, Warren wrote in his memoirs that this was the only incident he was aware of in which the Executive

Branch had illicitly tried to influence a Supreme Court decision. The chief justice was not aware of Fortas' work for the FBI and White House.

At least twenty cases possibly tainted by illegal ELSURs, including Muhammad Ali's and Jimmy Hoffa's cases, were awaiting the ruling. *Alderman* set forth the "standards and procedures" that the federal district courts were required to follow in determining whether criminal convictions were tainted when the FBI illegally intercepted conversations. The government was primarily concerned that criminal defendants in espionage cases do not obtain access to wiretap transcripts. The John Mitchell led Justice Department argued that the courts should trust the word of prosecutors that a particularly sensitive ELSUR (such as one directed at a foreign embassy) did not affect the fairness of the trial. This would put the defense at a disadvantage. Despite this, Justice Fortas dissented when it came to "national security material," activities specifically related to "acts of sabotage, espionage, or aggression by or on behalf of foreign states." These transcripts, he wrote, should not be "turned over to the defendant or his counsel for their scrutiny" when the "Attorney General has personally certified that specific portions of the unlawfully obtained materials are so sensitive that they should not be disclosed." Instead, the judge should review the materials in their chambers and decide, Fortas argued.

The Supreme Court rejected the government's position. The Court ruled that the FBI had to turn over the logs (the written transcripts) of the unlawful ELSUR to all criminal defendants, thus enabling defense lawyers to make informed arguments about whether the trial had been contaminated.

In *Street v. N.Y.*,[70] Justice Fortas again dissented, this case involving the burning of an American flag. "I have concluded that it is fair to say that the conviction was for the conduct of publicly burning the flag and not for the words used."[71] The majority disagreed. The Court overturned Street's conviction, finding he was punished for his words – "We don't need no damn flag" - and the flag burning.

Justice Fortas had a more expansive view of the First Amendment for students protesting the Vietnam War. He wrote the famous phrase that they do not "shed their constitutional rights to freedom of speech or expression at the schoolhouse gate."[72]

Worse days were on the horizon for Fortas. In 1966, stock manipulator Louis Wolfson had sent Justice Fortas a check for $20,000, purportedly for work with a foundation for social justice causes. Some in the Justice Department alleged that it was a payment to block a Securities Exchange Commission prosecution. Fortas paid the money back to the non-profit Wolfson Family Foundation during the same tax year. Reporter William Lambert broke the story in *Life* magazine.

Just prior to the damning article coming out, Hoover and Nixon discussed that the reporting was very strong. Eager to please the new president, Hoover told Nixon that he was "hoping to dig something up" on a possible real estate conflict of interest concerning Justice Fortas and liberal Federal Judge David Bazelon. Fortas should be off the Court, Nixon replied.[73]

This was just puffery by the director. Hoover did not need to dig something up. If Hoover was determined to get Fortas off the Court, his "O&C" files contained enough to destroy Fortas for repeatedly violating judicial ethics and for allegedly having sex with a teen.

DeLoach said, "Mr. Hoover took no action and made no comments concerning the resignation of Justice Fortas. [H]e meticulously avoided being involved in the matter."[74]

On May 14, 1969, Justice Fortas resigned from the Court, denying any wrongdoing associated with Wolfson. He became the first Supreme Court justice to resign in disgrace. But his greatest improprieties on the Court had not yet become known – nor would they, in his lifetime. For decades, the FBI would hide the evidence of Fortas' and its own unethical behavior from Congressional investigators, the press, and FOIA requesters. The sexual blackmail would stay hidden even longer. Finally, it took thirteen years, two lawyers and three FOIA lawsuits, to pry the file from the bowels of the J. Edgar Hoover Building.

CHAPTER 9: HISTORY VERSUS THE FBI. PLAYING THE FOIA INFORMATION GAME

The FBI has been maligned recently and falsely accused of all manner of conspiracies. One falsehood is that the Bureau instigated the entire January 6th insurrection at the United States Capitol.[75] Another is that G-men, along with the United States Department of Justice, colluded to frame former President Donald Trump for illegally possessing classified records at his Mar-a-Lago residence.[76]

Outlandish, wild accusations lacking in proof against the current FBI cannot be boot-strapped by the proven unconstitutional, lawless, and political behavior of the Bureau under Director J. Edgar Hoover.

The reality of the past reads like the plot of a fictional legal thriller: FBI Director J. Edgar Hoover uses a justice of the Supreme

Court of the United States in order to learn what the High Court is going to do, and to deflect blame, for warrantless FBI wiretapping cases. Not just any wiretapping cases. This electronic surveillance was done without a court order and impacted cases from Muhammad Ali to Jimmy Hoffa. A year later, this associate justice is approached by the FBI with an accusation of sexual impropriety. Don't worry, he's told. Your secret is safe with us . . .

It was a decade-long legal battle to wrest the once-secret documents from the FBI.

The FOIA was like a game. Imagine the Freedom of Information Act as a television game show. Say, "WHEEL-OF-FORTUNE"! Picture Vanna White, the silent, smiling model who launched a thousand vowels, in charge of information management at the Federal Bureau of Investigation. To play, address your request to Vanna at the J. Edgar Hoover building in Washington, D. C. There were 10,500 other requests queued up for a chance to look at 3.3 million pages of documents. How will this affect the book you are writing about how the FBI corrupted the supreme court?

Six years go by, WHEEL-OF-FORTUNE is popular. It is finally your turn. Rows of squares filled with thousands of blackened letters appear on a giant board. You must guess which squares hide the records you requested. Stand right there, next to the game show host and director of the FBI, Pat Sajak. Speak into the microphone. If you guessed correctly, Vanna would turn the card over and reveal the records - if they exist and are not subject to one of the nine statutory game show exemptions.

The rules of the game are complex, and your request must be precise. It is best if you have a lawyer standing by. Vanna is helpful up to a point, and you get boxes of documents no one else has ever seen. Some are heavily censored. Then Pat Sajak orders Vanna not to turn the card. You have to sue Vanna and Pat in federal court. It takes your lawsuit eight and a half years from the start to a partial settlement. You publish your book four years before the litigation is even close to ending. The book has some juicy revelations of official misconduct, but you still do not know what's behind the many rows of Wheel of Fortune squares. Vanna smiles her enigmatic information-Mona-Lisa smile. You are still curious. Your lawsuit is ongoing. You have played through three information dark ages overseen by Republicans. The Democratic president and his attorney general announce an information perestroika with a presumption in favor of disclosing information. The new openness allows you to settle large portions of your legal claims. Perky Vanna is gone, along with her Republican overseers, and the new document Hostess gives you a memo that the bad old FBI claimed you didn't even request.

The memo is from Hoover's super-secret stash of files he kept in his own office. It is a bombshell like something out of a John Grisham novel. One of the justices and FBI informer himself, might have been blackmailed by allegations of having sex with a teen by J. Edgar, who himself had been hounded by questions about his sexuality. That would have made an explosive addition to your book. It has been thirteen years since you requested this information.

Trying to obtain FBI records using the Freedom of Information Act is not supposed to be like a TV game show. After thirteen years seeking the FBI's documentation of its relationship with the Supreme Court and its justices - eight of those years spent in litigation - we have found that while the process can be just as much *fun* as a game show, it might yield less reliable results.[77]

REAL "X-FILES": THE TRUTH IS OUT THERE (MAYBE)

The FBI, with television agents Fox Mulder and Dana Scully in pursuit, really does maintain X-Files, records containing scandalous secrets of historical significance that it holds dear and prefers not to release.[78] Some of these secrets are neither exempt from the FOIA nor properly classifiable. This chapter recounts my series of FOIA requests, through the morass of FBI bureaucracy, on to the shoals of federal litigation, and finally to the receipt of decades old memos about the alleged sexual activity of a Supreme Court justice.

Considering the wording of the Freedom of Information Act, 5 U.S.C. 552, a FOIA request would seem to be a straightforward and efficient tool for historical research. One need only request all FBI records about a particular justice or the Supreme Court, and twenty days later a package (these days it's an email) would be sent containing all the FBI documents necessary to write the desired history.

Unfortunately, it never worked that way. To begin with, the FOIA exempts nine categories of information from mandatory disclosure. These exemptions are subject to interpretation and are quite nettlesome to apply. As a practical matter an agency might not be able to review documents and separate out the non-exempt information within a time frame remotely close to the time period mandated by the FOIA.

For another thing, it is simply not in the perceived self-interest of a secretive agency, such as the FBI, to release sensitive information that may subject it, or persons with whom it has had dealings, to controversy or criticism. There is certainly a degree of internal bridling against the FOIA, and some degree of covert resistance against its requirements by the very officials responsible for its implementation.

I first began research about the FBI and the Supreme Court in 1983, one year out of law school. I submitted a FOI request for all FBI records on Chief Justice Earl Warren, Associate Justice William O. Douglas, and the FBI surveillance of the U.S. Supreme Court. In response to my repeated follow up letters, FBI officials finally informed me in May 1984 that my request about the Supreme Court was not specific enough. So, I tried again; "I am requesting a complete search of all filing systems and locations for records... pertaining to the United States Supreme Court as a body."[79] Since this broad request about the High Court seemed to be difficult for the FBI to process, I also asked for all FBI records on Justices Fortas, Felix Frankfurter, and Hugo Black and on other specified federal judges and court personnel.

In response, the head of the FBI's records management division wrote me on September 4, 1984: "search of the indices to our central records system files at FBI headquarters did not reveal any pertinent information on the United States Supreme Court as a body."[80] What I did not know at the time was that on August 6, 1984, an FBI employee (possibly the same one who prepared the September 4 letter) had checked the FBI's general indices[81] and had located three main files and five cross references to the "United States Supreme Court," including a document called "United States Supreme Court law clerks." The latter file pertained to an alleged "left-wing ring" of clerks. This was itself just one serial in – a two-thousand-page file containing a variety of information on the Supreme Court. The FBI's general indices listed this file under the heading "Supreme Court."[82]

I found out about this 2000-page trove of records about the High Court only because Bureau officials had sent me, apparently by mistake, part of an internal memorandum that described who I was, what I was doing, and the type of information I was being provided. I later learned that such documents are called "high visibility memoranda." They are generated as part of the FBI FOIA Section efforts to anticipate and minimize negative publicity resulting from FOIA releases, including prerelease information to family members of the subject of the request. Thus prompted, I requested my own FBI file, which I received in 1987 after a three-year delay. This file totaled some 900 pages of correspondence, search slips (which revealed the search prompts used in the files located as the result of the search) and internal memoranda, which showed that FBI personnel had indeed located as early as 1984 both main files and cross references on the Supreme Court at the very time I was being told that the FBI maintained no such records. This discovery, in turn, prompted me to request previously "overlooked" files.

Five days before sending the letter denying that any "pertinent" information on the court existed, some of these files had been described in an "internal fee waiver memorandum," which means that the records had been located and slated for release. This memo, dated August 30, 1984, describes various files that were about to be released to me, for the consideration of a committee, including chief of the Freedom of Information Section, James K. Hall, that would decide whether or not I would be granted a waiver of the usual copying fees due to the historical and public interest in the records. The memorandum included the information that three main files comprising about one hundred pages on the Supreme Court had been located, including two pages on extortion letters mailed to the court, and one file on a 1974 FBI investigation of leaks to newspapers of sensitive information about court personnel. The fee waiver committee met on October 30, 1984, decided the records were of substantial public interest, and granted me a fifty percent reduction of the usual copying fees.[83] This happened five days before I was told the records on the Supreme Court did not exist.

I ultimately requested FBI files on every deceased Supreme Court Justice going back to the early part of the 1900s as a way to pry loose whatever records related to the High Court as a body. I also requested another large file entitled "Federal Judges," 62-53025, which contained miscellaneous information on relations between the FBI and various members of the judiciary going back some fifty years.

My new request prompted a phone call, on August 11, 1987, from Helen Near, an employee of the FBI FOI-PA Section. When processing one of my requests she informed me an entire file about the Supreme Court had been located. The file totaled 1200 pages expanded to some two thousand pages when a newspaper clippings appendix was added. Did I want it? This ultimately proved to be headquarters file 62-27585, consisting of reams of documents, including the memo on the left-wing law clerks, and a file proving high-level court employees served as FBI informers in the 1950s. The left-wing clerks file was identified on the August 6th, 1984, search slip as the seventy-fourth serial in this file.

As of that time, the FBI had released enough information to enable me to write several articles on individual justices and the Bureau. However, I had yet to receive the FBI's largest file on the Supreme Court, and it appeared that FBI officials were determined to ignore my other requests for a search of the

Bureau's electronic surveillance indices, as well as "Special File Rooms," "Do Not File" and "Official and Confidential." With the J. Roderick MacArthur Foundation, Dick Goldensohn Fund, and the Institute for Southern Studies now providing financial support, I found myself an attorney, and in March 1980 we filed a complaint in the Greensboro, N.C. federal courthouse.

In response to our initial flurry of motions, Justice Department lawyers filed an answer that said basically I should be sent packing. My lawyer, Paul M. Green, was advised that if I withdraw all my pending motions, I would be invited to FBI headquarters in Washington, D.C., for a "special tour" of the FBI FOIA section. I could then talk with an FBI representative about how I might better frame my FOIA requests. Their view seemed to be that I was trying to make a career out of requesting FBI records but had been shooting myself in the foot by misframing my FOIA requests.

We declined their offer. However, our aggressive litigation strategy seemed to be having all the effect of shooting spitballs at the hind quarters of a fossilized brontosaurus. We were particularly disappointed that the court would not allow pretrial discovery into the FBI's policies and procedures for complying with the FOIA itself. Nonetheless, Paul believed that such information was required to be kept publicly available under the subsection of the FOIA, whether or not it was formally requested. Because the FBI was not complying with this other subsection, Paul and I exchanged hats. I, acting as his lawyer, filed suit in the U.S. District Court for the Eastern District of North Carolina in Raleigh, where Paul maintained his law office. During the ensuing two years in court, we obtained thousands of pages of internal FBI memoranda dating back to the FOIA's inception, plus an injunction requiring the FBI to maintain and make available to the general public a current edition of its Freedom of Information-Privacy Act manual at the reading room at FBI headquarters in Washington, DC, as well as a court order for attorney's fees even though the judge denied a motion for frivolous litigation sanctions against the government attorneys.

The FBI took the ridiculous position that it was not an "agency" within the meaning of the FOIA despite a federal regulation explicitly requiring the FBI to place its policy materials in the J. Edgar Hoover building reading room. The idea of making a career out of suing the FBI was beginning to have a certain charm.

The FOI-PA manual shed little light on Hoover's "Official and Confidential" ("O&C") files, which had been the bone of contention from the outset. We had argued that the 18,000-page collection of Hoover's most private records must be searched page by page for references to the supreme court and its justices. In response, the FBI had steadfastly maintained that Hoover's "O&C" files were fully integrated within the FBI's general indices, and thus no special search was required.

On March 28th, 1989, Judge N. Carlton Tilley held a hearing to inquire into this and other matters. Three FBI agents, including Chris Flynn and Angus Llewellyn, attended from Washington. Flynn addressed the court about my request concerning Hoover's "O&C" files, conceding for arguments sake that "there may be a mother lode of information that Mr. Charns is interested in." The problem was accessing these files. The only index, Flynn said, was the FBI's general indices and the electronic surveillance index, which were set up for the convenience of the FBI, not FOIA requesters.

We later found out that this was not exactly true. Hoover's "O&C" files contains an index to the 164 folders contained therein. The index lists the name of four supreme court justices, all of whom were the subjects of my FOIA request then under litigation.

Even without this knowledge, we convinced Judge Tilley that the FBI had not proved that its search for records was adequate. He ruled that the FBI's exemption claims would have to be reviewed *in camera*, in the judge's chambers, without our presence. He then appointed U.S. Magistrate-Judge Russell Eliason to serve as special master. Eliason set a relaxed timetable. It would take more than eighteen months for the FBI to process records and file declarations establishing that it had complied with the FOIA.

The FBI was forced to state under oath the details of its search for records and why they claimed that they didn't have records which their own files proved they had in their possession.

The FBI responded: "Upon review of the actual documents by FOI-PA personnel, these references were found not to be pertinent to the Supreme Court as a body, thus plaintiff [Charns] was advised by letter dated September 5, 1984, that the FBI had no responsive records. . . . In handling the related request for plaintiff, an employee in the FOI-PA section became aware that the FBI had records indexed under 'Supreme Court.' It then became apparent that the indices search done on Plaintiff's May 17, 1984, request was not sufficient. It can only be surmised that the search was done on 'United States Supreme Court' and not 'Supreme Court.' . . . This was not according to the way the search should have been conducted. However, once the existence of the files was discovered, an employee of the FBI telephonically notified the plaintiff of the existence of these records on August 11, 1987. It is important to note, the FBI informed plaintiff of this apparent mistake." [84]

The court ultimately accepted this explanation of a seemingly innocent mistake. There are some obvious problems with this. To begin with, my May 17, 1984, request was clearly intended to be as inclusive as possible, and it was unreasonable for the FBI employee to decide unilaterally that the eight files subsequently located were "not pertinent" to my request, without even informing me of their existence. Second, if the actual documents were in fact reviewed in 1984, it must have been seen that the reference to Supreme Court clerks, 62-27585-74, was just a small part of a 2000-page file on the Supreme Court, 62-27585. Third, the fact that a fee waiver memorandum was prepared, and a fee waiver approved shows that at least someone in that FBI FOI-PA section had determined back in 1984 that at least one hundred pages and three main files were pertinent to my request and should have been released to me at a reduced copying rate. Finally, although the FBI did ultimately inform me of the existence of the Supreme Court file, 62-27585, this disclosure never would have happened had I not requested specific material from that file, thus making my discovery of it inevitable. In addition, I had requested the Supreme Court file by its exact file number.

One positive outcome, the FBI finally released its file entitled "Supreme Court," which showed, among other revelations, that three highly placed court employees served as FBI sources of information during the 1950s Then, out of the blue, in December 1989, the FBI released to me memoranda dealing with the FBI's 1966 approach to Justice Fortas regarding a criminal case then pending before the Supreme Court. These memos were the first indications that Justice Fortas had served as an FBI informer while on the High Court. Subsequent research indicated that the FBI's contact with Fortas may have influenced the High Court's deliberation in cases involving illegal electronic surveillance. Although the memos had clearly come from Hoover's "O&C" files and were responsive to my FOIA request, the FBI steadfastly continued to maintain that it had no obligation to find the memos and give them to me. The memos were being provided "as a courtesy." In addition to the "courtesy" copies of memoranda long kept secret at FBI headquarters, Bureau officials produced many pages of records under a court supervised scheduling order. In 1991, Magistrate-Judge Eliason issued his recommendation: some of the FOIA-exemption claims would be upheld, some would be overruled, and FBI would have to provide better evidence that Hoover's "O&C" files had been properly indexed and the indices adequately searched.

There the case sat for five years. Except for occasional correspondence, we all went on to other things. I finished my book.

Pending lawsuits, however, have many annoying qualities, one of which is that they very seldom go away all by themselves. Eventually, Judge Tilley reviewed the magistrate-judge's recommendation, upheld most of it and set a date by which the FBI had to comply.

As a July 26, 1996, hearing date approached, Paul reviewed everything the FBI had ever submitted about Hoover's "O&C" files and prepared a memorandum to the court relying almost entirely on the FBI's own statements. These included admissions such as the FOI- PA Section chief's 1989 letter to me stating that information in Hoover's "O&C" files was "not separately retrievable through our indices." Or a declaration on file with the court in which Agent Llewellyn stated under oath that "page by page review of the voluminous Hoover "O&C" files would have been necessary to locate the specific references to Fortas." We also studied the actual index to the Hoover "O&C" files which had been sent to me by Professor Athan Theoharis, another FOIA requester. Only a few folder titles were blacked out. By now, all but perhaps 1000 pages of Hoover's "O&C" files had been made public at least in part - including files entitled "Frankfurter, Felix," "Jackson, Robert H," "Murphy, Attorney General Frank."

But the index had an important clue. Paul noticed that one of the blacked-out titles, folder 71, happened to fall right between folder 70 ("Foreign Influence in the Black Extremist Movement" and folder 72 (Foxworth, P. E") In addition, the black censor-marks for folder 71 was exactly eleven letters, the exact number of letters, comma and space in FORTAS, ABE. Elated, we pointed out our discovery in a memorandum to the court, hopeful that this would clinch our motion for a page-by-page search of the "O&C" files.

Days before the hearing, the government's lawyer admitted that indeed, folder 71 was entitled Abe Fortas. When we arrived at the courthouse in Greensboro, Julia Eichorst, an FBI FOIA analyst, handed me the folder documenting a sexual allegation against a sitting Supreme Court justice. There was no claim that the material was being provided merely as a courtesy.

Decades after that day in federal court, in 2024, forty-one years after I initially requested the FBI's files on Justice Fortas, I made a request to The National Archives for folder 71, Fortas, Abe, Hoover's "O&C" files. It took them less than a week to release it to me after my e-FOIA request. This version was more complete. It had fewer redactions where the censor denied access to information using one of the nine statutory exemptions.

I learned that it was the office manager at Fortas' former law firm who had introduced him to the teenager who would accuse him of once forbidden, illegal, sexual encounters. The additional details clarified some things and made others murkier. The more heavily redacted memo made it appear that Fortas knew his accuser. Now that does not seem clear.

In 2024, I made an additional e-FOIA request to the FBI for folder 71. They told me it was on the public website with other Abe Fortas files. That wasn't true. As I write this, my appeal of this FBI misdirection is on appeal to the U.S. Department of Justice. Forty-one years after my initial request, the Bureau is still giving me the run around. I want to compare the three versions of folder 71.

Why did the FBI stonewall for thirteen (or forty-one) years? Because they were allowed to. Because they can. Rarely do historians or journalists sue. Sanctions, such as financial penalties or contempt of court against FBI attorneys or staff are almost unheard of. But winning is expensive and time-consuming. The litigation tactics used against me by the U.S. Justice Department attorneys and FBI employees on behalf of the Bureau were unprofessional and lacked the candor required of attorneys, special agents, or government officials.

Recommendations in my 1992 book included that the FOIA should be strengthened by Congress. I still believe that. In addition, I noted a basic problem with FBI background checks of justices and judges. "[A]n FBI report on a [Supreme Court] nominee's background should be viewed with a much skepticism as reports submitted by other interest groups. Regarding the Supreme Court, the FBI was, is, and will remain an interested party that serves the president."[85] This proved itself true in the Brett Kavanaugh confirmation battle. The FBI did as little as the White House requested.[86] Some 4,000 tips went uninvestigated.[87]

A secretive law enforcement agency with a sordid history can never be trusted. Vigorous Congressional oversight, a vigilant and independent media, and the aggressive use of FOIA requests and litigation is required.[88]

FINAL THOUGHTS

Sometimes writing about our ugly legal history makes me feel ashamed to be a lawyer. Our country's past, the sin and scandal of our government's hateful anti-gay bigotry, is painful.

Even in law school I wondered if I was cut out to be a lawyer. I knew that I wouldn't work in a big firm or make the big bucks doing corporate law. Criminal and constitutional law was what I wanted to do. That and investigate corruption in the legal system.

I was fresh out of law school. Pulitzer Prize-winning historian David J. Garrow taught me to recognize FBI Director J. Edgar Hoover's looping crossed initials in the files on the Supreme Court that I was amassing. That was over four decades ago. The hunt for proof of the FBI's misconduct with respect to the High Court hooked me. It became a life-long pursuit. I didn't foresee the extent to which the justices themselves would participate so willingly in the institution's sacking and undermining. Both liberals and conservatives on the Court all vied for the ethical bottom. The championship of institutional degradation. Today, the right-wing of the Court is winning the Unethical Legal Olympics. In 1966, it was a rising-star liberal justice doing the damage along with his Democrat president. Corruption is an equal opportunity venture.

Writing and researching this book has been a challenge for me. I wondered if it was ethical or moral for me to name Hoover's victims. Fortas.[89] Bartlett. George. Couldn't they all simply be in their graves without an attorney/journalist reporting on their alleged sex lives? I considered not naming Bartlett. Fortas, I didn't consider in the same light. He was a public figure during his life. For the other two, private citizens all their lives, did I have the right to out them?

At one point I considered going to confession about my concerns. Was this the sin of scandal? If it was, the entire book was filled with it. The behavior of many of the actors in the book was scandalous. I decided that I am simply a scribe, reporting about government misbehavior. Even though I am a repressed Roman Catholic well into AARP age, confessing that I was writing truthful albeit disturbing history was not sinful. Talking about this in a confessional was silly. After all, as a criminal defense attorney, my ability to justify my legal arguments and trial strategies was highly developed.

I decided to publish Bartlett's name and refer to Fortas' accuser as George. I felt the story lacked authenticity if I withheld the actual names of real people, the adults, even though they had their sexual privacy invaded by the FBI. I acknowledge that the government ruined many lives in this very same way.

Would I have similar anguish if the allegations were of heterosexual sex outside marriage? Was this a sign of my own bigotry? My own religion's teaching about the LGBTQ+ community is odious to me and has harmed untold numbers of faithful, observant gay Catholics. When I was a first-year student in college, I left the Church for this reason. I returned, more than seven years later, after I graduated from law school.

I surveyed my family and one close friend about my decision to name Hoover's victims. Each made reasonable arguments for and against doing so. What about any surviving family or friends of either man? Bartlett married and divorced according to Ancestry.com. Would I be doing harm or causing someone pain a half century later? Could the FBI memo even be trusted? What did I want my writing legacy to be?

The final decision was mine. Presenting the facts as I uncovered them won out. Fighting so long, and so hard for these records influenced my decision. These records are publicly available in The National Archives. I also made the decision to attach folder 71 and the Fred Black folder as an Appendix to this book with Geoge's middle and last name redacted. I wanted to make sure that the original documents were accessible to readers and researchers alike. You can make up your own mind about my conclusions, motives, and decisions.

ACKNOWLEDGEMENTS

Thank you to Paul M. Green, my FOIA attorney, collaborator, and friend. Thanks to Tucker Charns for editorial input. Thanks to Laurel Goldman and all the great folks in her writing workshop: Chrys Bullard, David Halperin, David Levine, and Martha Pentecost.

I am very grateful to Michael J. Hancock, Archives Specialist at The National Archives, who did in four days what it took the FBI decades to do.
Thanks Patricia Ford, word wizard.

The cover photo of Abe Fortas and LBJ in 1965 is courtesy of the LBJ Library. Artistic modifications to that photo by mac.

OTHER BOOKS BY THIS AUTHOR

Praise for: "*Cloak and Gavel* . . . is the product of an eight-year struggle to force the FBI to reveal its Supreme Court snooping. Charns got . . . hard evidence that Hoover attempted to monitor the court's private deliberations and manipulate some of the justices." Wall Street Journal, A13, 9/1/92

"The FBI's scandalous techniques ranged from illegal wiretapping, to disinformation campaigns, to using Justice Abe Fortas as a Bureau informant." Harvard Law Review, Vol 106, p. 812.

"[A] bonanza of Supreme Court history, providing depth and perspective to some great cases of our time." St Louis Post-Dispatch, 10/18/92.

"Charns is a renowned civil libertarian. [I]n 'How Hockey Saved the World,' Charns takes a tongue-in-cheek view of politics and sports, delivering humor and laughs that recall the work of Mark Twain, Joseph Heller and Ambrose Bierce." Cliff Bellamy,
Durham Herald-Sun June 2006. [T]he author's subversive wit and genuine belief in the game's magic are oddly persuasive. An amiable meditation to warm even the iciest hearts." Kirkus Discoveries 7/7/06.

The Girl Who Wore A Hockey Helmet: **In this winning legal thriller from Charns (author of the series), public defender "Star" Katazyna Gwiazda in Randleman County, NC, faces a world of troubles, the biggest of which is her arrest for allegedly murdering a local judge. Unfortunately, Star has good reason to dislike the judge and was in the middle of defending a difficult client in his court. She also is trying to navigate through personal problems while continuing to defend low-level miscreants. As her own case proceeds, she finds corruption among tight connections in the small town and her only hope may be her collection of offbeat friends and colleagues.

The real joy of this book [*The Girl Who Wore A Hockey Helmet*] is Charns' collection of eccentric characters, who lend engaging color but always remain believable. The author is, himself, a criminal defense attorney, and has a keen eye and ear for the small southern town milieu, such as when Star's friend Joy gets righteously angry when her married boyfriend tells her he's going back to his wife—the next morning. The courtroom scenes are lively and believable, and the deft cross-examination scenes keep the pages turning. ... Charns keeps everything moving briskly to a satisfying ending.

Star is a delightful character, an engaging mix of bravado and self-doubt, prescribed with lithium for manic-depression—a sleuth with realistically depicted mental health challenges is refreshing. Star is honest with herself and the reader about her condition and neither glorifies nor dramatizes it—describing the side effects that sometimes are worse than the diagnosis. She's also upfront about her awkward love life, which lends a welcome note of pathos to the courtroom shenanigans, and readers are left hoping to meet this imperfect but lovable lawyer in a future adventure. Publisher Weekly Booklife Review

Other books by Alex Charns include, *Bones of Black Saints*, *Barrio Butterfly*, *Ka-Boom*? and *Listening to Chopin While Fighting Nazis*, all published by Bull City Law Publishing, Durham, NC.

APPENDIX OF SELECTED FBI DOCUMENTS RECEIVED IN CHARNS V. U.S. DEPT. OF JUSTICE

FOLDER 71, ABE FORTAS, HOOVER'S "O&C" FILES

FOLDER 71, ABE FORTAS, HOOVER'S "O&C" FILES from the National Archives

FRED BLACK FOLDER, HOOVER'S "O&C" FILES

```
                FEDERAL BUREAU OF INVESTIGATION

                Room 5744_____, 1967
        _____
        TO:
                                        ┌─────────────────┐
            ✓  Director                  │ Mr. Tolson  ✓   │
           ___ Mr. DeLoach               │ Mr. DeLoach     │
           ___ Mr. Mohr                  │ Mr. Mohr        │
           ___ Mr. Wick                  │ Mr. Wick        │
           ___ Mr. Gale                  │ Mr. Casper      │
           ___ Mr. Rosen                 │ Mr. Callahan    │
           ___ Mr. Callahan              │ Mr. Conrad      │
           ___ Mr. Casper                │ Mr. Felt        │
           ___ Mr. Conrad                │ Mr. Gale        │
           ___ Mr. Felt                  │ Mr. Rosen       │
           ___ Mr. Sullivan              │ Mr. Sullivan    │
           ___ Mr. Tavel                 │ Mr. Tavel       │
           ___ Mr. Trotter               │ Mr. Trotter     │
           ___ Mr. Beaver                │ Tele. Room      │
           ___ Miss Gandy                │ Miss Holmes     │
           ___ Miss Holmes               │ Miss Gandy  ✓   │
           ___ Personnel Files Section   │           oL.   │
           ___ Records Branch            └─────────────────┘
           ___ Mrs. Skillman
           ___ Mrs. Brown
           ___ John Quander

        See Me              For appropriate action
        Send File           Note and Return
        Please Call Me

        _____

        _____

        _____

        _____

        _____

                              _____
                                  Clyde Tolson
```

7/20/67

Attached memorandum from the Washington Field Office reflects possible homosexual activities on the part of Justice Abe Fortas.

Messrs. Tolson and DeLoach recommend that a memorandum be prepared forwarding this information to the Attorney General.

CDD:CSH

No. DeLoach should call Fortas. H

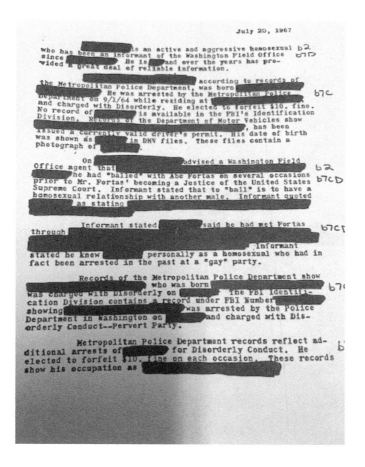

July 24, 1967

MR. TOLSON:

Pursuant to the Director's instructions, I saw Justice Fortas at his home at 5:10 p.m. on 7/24/67. I told him we had received an allegation from a source of information reflecting participation in homosexual activities on his part. I stated that the Director wanted this matter discreetly and informally brought to his attention so that he would be aware of such an allegation. I mentioned that the FBI was taking no further action in connection with this matter and that the fact that the Director was making this available to him was strictly for his own personal protection and knowledge.

Justice Fortas was handed the attached memorandum so that he could read it personally. After reading this memorandum, he told me that the charges were ridiculous and absolutely false. He stated he had never committed a homosexual act in his life and while he might be properly accused of normal sexual relations while a young man and during his married life, he most certainly had never committed homosexual acts at any time.

With respect to the arrest record of one ▓▓▓▓▓▓ who has been arrested on three different occasions by the Metropolitan Police for homosexual activity, Justice Fortas told me he wasn't surprised to learn of this inasmuch as he and ▓▓▓▓▓▓ always felt a little suspicious toward ▓▓▓▓▓▓ and has served in this capacity for the past five years. Justice Fortas stated that he and ▓▓▓▓▓▓ in the past, have noted that ▓▓▓▓▓▓ seems to be somewhat effeminate and that he never tried to date the girls ▓▓▓▓▓▓. While not making any commitment, Justice Fortas stated that ▓▓▓▓▓▓ arrest record could certainly prove most embarrassing to ▓▓▓▓▓▓ and that something would have to be done about the situation.

Justice Fortas expressed great appreciation for having been provided with the above facts. He asked that his thanks be extended to the Director for having handled the matter in this manner. There followed a brief discussion concerning the racial situation in Detroit inasmuch as Justice Fortas has been at the White House all day at the President's request, working on this matter.

Respectfully,

C. D. DeLOACH

Enclosure
CDD:hmg
1 - DeLoach

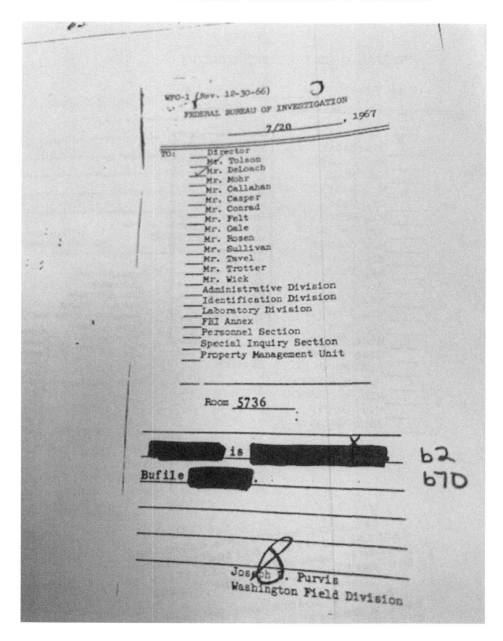

FEDERAL BUREAU OF INVESTIGATION

Room 5744 _____, 1967

TO:

- ✓ Director
- Mr. DeLoach
- Mr. Mohr
- Mr. Wick
- Mr. Gale
- Mr. Rosen
- Mr. Callahan
- Mr. Casper
- Mr. Conrad
- Mr. Felt
- Mr. Sullivan
- Mr. Tavel
- Mr. Trotter
- Mr. Beaver
- Miss Gandy
- Miss Holmes
- Personnel Files Section
- Records Branch
- Mrs. Skillman
- Mrs. Brown
- John Quander

Mr. Tolson
Mr. DeLoach
Mr. Mohr
Mr. Wick
Mr. Casper
Mr. Callahan
Mr. Conrad
Mr. Felt
Mr. Gale
Mr. Rosen
Mr. Sullivan
Mr. Tavel
Mr. Trotter
Tele. Room
Miss Holmes
Miss Gandy ✓

7/20/67

Attached memorandum from the Washington Field Office reflects possible homosexual activities on the part of Justice Abe Fortas.

Messrs. Tolson and DeLoach recommend that a memorandum be prepared forwarding this information to the Attorney General.

CDD:CSH

	Mr. Tolson _____
	Mr. DeLoach _____
	Mr. Mohr _____
	Mr. Wick _____
	Mr. Casper _____
	Mr. Callahan _____
July 24, 1967	Mr. Conrad _____
	Mr. Felt _____
	Mr. Gale _____
MR. TOLSON:	Mr. Rosen _____
	Mr. Sullivan _____
	Mr. Tavel _____
	Mr. Trotter _____
	Tele. Room _____
	Miss Holmes _____
	Miss Gandy ✓

Pursuant to the Director's instructions, I saw Justice Fortas at his home at 5:10 p.m. on 7/24/67. I told him we had received an allegation from a source of information reflecting participation in homosexual activities on his part. I stated that the Director wanted this matter discreetly and informally brought to his attention so that he would be aware of such an allegation. I mentioned that the FBI was taking no further action in connection with this matter and that the fact that the Director was making this available to him was strictly for his own personal protection and knowledge.

Justice Fortas was handed the attached memorandum so that he could read it personally. After reading this memorandum, he told me that the charges were ridiculous and absolutely false. He stated he had never committed a homosexual act in his life and while he might be properly accused of normal sexual relations while a young man and during his married life, he most certainly had never committed homosexual acts at any time.

With respect to the arrest record of one William Norris Bartlett, who has been arrested on three different occasions by the Metropolitan Police for homosexual activity, Justice Fortas told me he wasn't surprised to learn of this inasmuch as he and the other partners of his former law firm always felt a little suspicious toward Bartlett. Bartlett is the office manager of this law firm and has served in this capacity for the past five years. He supervises the work of approximately 50 female employees. Justice Fortas stated that he and Attorneys Porter and Arnold, in the past, have noted that Bartlett seems to be somewhat effeminate and that he never tried to date the girls in the office. While not making any commitment, Justice Fortas stated that Bartlett's arrest record could certainly prove most embarrassing to the law firm and that something would have to be done about the situation.

Justice Fortas expressed great appreciation for having been provided with the above facts. He asked that his thanks be extended to the Director for having handled the matter in this manner. There followed a brief discussion concerning the racial situation in Detroit inasmuch as Justice Fortas has been at the White House all day at the President's request, working on this matter.

Respectfully,

C. D. DeLOACH

Enclosure
CDD:hmm
1 - DeLoach

UNITED STATES DEPARTMENT OF JUSTICE
FEDERAL BUREAU OF INVESTIGATION
WASHINGTON 25, D. C.

JUL 5 1967

J. Edgar Hoover, Director

The following FBI record, NUMBER 329 951 D, is furnished FOR OFFICIAL USE ONLY.

CONTRIBUTOR OF FINGERPRINTS	NAME AND NUMBER	ARRESTED OR RECEIVED	CHARGE	DISPOSITION
Air Force	William Norris Bartlett #AF 13 419 344	9-4-51		
PD Redwood City Calif	William Norris Bartlett #10773	appl 1-21-55		
PD Wash DC	William Norris Bartlett #173597	11-7-59	DC pervert party	

Notations indicated by * ARE NOT BASED ON FINGERPRINTS IN FBI files. The notations are based on data formerly furnished this Bureau concerning individuals of the same or similar names or aliases and ARE LISTED ONLY AS INVESTIGATIVE LEADS.

FOIA(b)2
FOIA(b)7 - (D)

July 20, 1967

[REDACTED] is an active and aggressive homosexual who has been an informant of the Washington Field Office since June, 1963. He is 28 and over the years has provided a great deal of reliable information.

[FOIA(b)7 - (C)]

On 7/18/67, [REDACTED] advised a Washington Field Office agent that [FOIA(b)7 - (C)] had told the informant he had "balled" with Abe Fortas on several occasions prior to Mr. Fortas' becoming a Justice of the United States Supreme Court. Informant stated that to "ball" is to have a homosexual relationship with another male. Informant quoted [FOIA(b)7 - (C)] as stating he felt it was "convenient to have Miss Fortas on the bench."

Informant stated [FOIA(b) - (C)] said he had met Fortas through William Bartlett, an associate of [FOIA(b)7 - (C)] who is employed by the law firm of Arnold and Porter, the firm with which Justice Fortas was formerly associated. Informant stated he knew Bartlett personally as a homosexual who had in fact been arrested in the past at a "gay" party.

Records of the Metropolitan Police Department show William Norris Bartlett, who was born 8/25/34 in Washington, was charged with Disorderly on 11/7/59. The FBI Identification Division contains a record under FBI Number 329 951 D showing William Norris Bartlett was arrested by the Police Department in Washington on 11/7/59 and charged with Disorderly Conduct--Pervert Party.

Metropolitan Police Department records reflect additional arrests of Bartlett for Disorderly Conduct. He elected to forfeit $10. fine on each occasion. These records show his occupation as "Legal Secretary, Manager."

ALEX CHARNS

METROPOLITAN POLICE DEPARTMENT

NAME: BARTLETT William Norris
ADDRESS: 2013 N. H. Ave. N.W.

RACE: W X MARRIED
       C   DIVORCED   DEAD X
       FB SINGLE X

BIRTHPLACE: D. C.   9   25   1934

Mother's Name: Lydia Pitts
Father's Name: Norris
Occupation: Legal Secretary; Manager

PCT	CASE NO.	DATE	AGE	OFFENSE	COMPLAINANT	OFFICER	DISPOSITIONS
MD	3532	11-7-59	25	Disorderly	AC Fair	Brewer FW	IF 510
				4663 Kendrick Rd Suitland Md DB DC 8-25-34 m. Sydia			C. Norris
3	3942	9-19-61	27	disorderly	C E Minnick	Minnick	
		1-19-62	29				
		13-19-62	29	disorderly		M: Ledia	F: Norris
				7530 Ambergate Pl Va. DC 8-25-34			
3	3767	7-16-67	33	Disorderly	D Farmer	Farmer	

METROPOLITAN POLICE DEPARTMENT, Washington, D. C.

NAME: ____ George
ADDRESS: 1313 M St. NW

RACE: WHITE X MARRIED   SINGLE X
      NEGRO   DIVORCED   WIDOWED
      OTHER   SEX: MALE X FEMALE

BIRTHPLACE: DC   MONTH 7 DAY 7 YEAR 1947

Mother's Maiden Name: Bellie
Father's Name: ____
Occupation: Laborer

CT.	CASE NO.	DATE	AGE	OFFENSE	COMPLAINANT	OFFICER	DISPOSITIONS
	14687	9/1/64	18	disorderly	T Marshall	RA Eias	

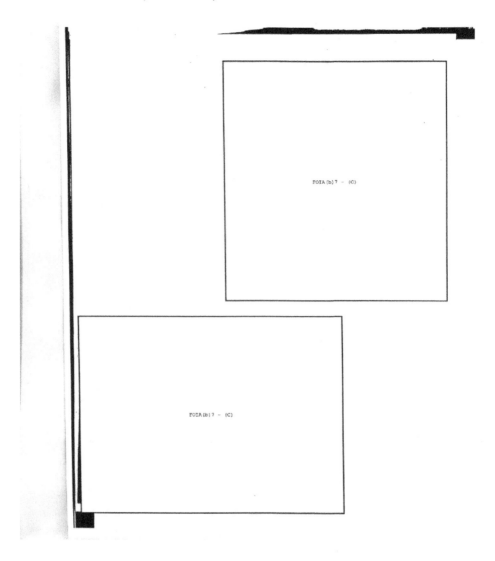

Return to Miss Gandy for filing.

UNITED STATES DEPARTMENT OF JUSTICE
FEDERAL BUREAU OF INVESTIGATION
WASHINGTON, D.C. 20535

10:15 AM

June 14, 1966

MEMORANDUM FOR PERSONAL FILES

Assistant to the Director DeLoach called and stated Supreme Court Justice Abe Fortas returned his call last night and asked him to have breakfast with the Justice this morning. Mr. DeLoach stated he outlined to the Justice the entire Black matter and told him what it is necessary for us to do is to protect the Bureau and gave the Justice the background of the exchange of correspondence and how Attorney General Katzenbach tried to blacken our name. Mr. DeLoach stated he mentioned to the Justice and showed him a copy of the New York telephone letter approved by former Attorney General Kennedy and the memorandum advising the Department of the use of microphones and trespass. Mr. DeLoach told the Justice that with respect to the Black case, despite all the facts we were going to furnish the Attorney General, no doubt they would furnish the Supreme Court a slanted version of the matter. Justice Fortas said he recognized this fact and that actually what this boils down to is a fight for the Presidency; that Bobby Kennedy has been trying to knock Vice President Humphrey out with the liberals and this is a continuation and Kennedy should be exposed.

Mr. DeLoach stated Justice Fortas asked if we had furnished the information to the President and was told we had for the most part but the President could not be involved in furnishing information to the Supreme Court. Fortas said the problem is to get the facts to the Supreme Court and the people and to protect the FBI and then referred to the Black Case and said after it had been ineptly and inadequately presented by that "dumb" Thurgood Marshall, there was a confidential meeting among the Justices of the Supreme Court and even though he, Fortas, planned to disqualify himself, he attended and gave his opinions and Justice Byron White was there and did not like what was taking place and was trying to defend Bobby Kennedy. Fortas stated that after the meeting, the Justices decided if they remanded the Black Case to a lower court, Katzenbach would merely pick a patsy as a Federal Judge and try the case in favor of the Federal Government and Katzenbach and he said the Supreme Court Justices did not want that done but Justices Douglas and Black, particularly, wanted to set themselves up as a tribunal to get further information and wanted to know who authorized it. Fortas said the Court can do either of two things: can either remand it to a lower court or issue a directed verdict for the defendant.

Memorandum for Personal Files — June 14, 1966

Fortas said he did not see how they could take the latter course of action because this particular microphone information had no relevancy insofar as the tax case is concerned. Fortas said it boils down to the fact that we have to get these facts out somehow rather than Katzenbach taking it and presenting a slanted version. Fortas said he thought he should slip over and talk to the President before he leaves for Florida and tell the President it is a continuing fight for the Presidency and it will be injurious to the President and other individuals and the country. Fortas said that obviously Mr. Hoover cannot go up and testify before the Supreme Court counteracting what Katzenbach is furnishing as it would be bad insofar as the country and history is concerned. Fortas said what he can do is prevail upon the President to appoint an arbitrator who will defend Johnson and take the evidence as furnished by the FBI and show it in a fair light and have this man sit down and listen to the FBI and take this damning evidence, which is on record, and write a report and let this stand as the answer to the Supreme Court and the Court will get all the facts and can remand it to a lower court and the FBI will be protected. Fortas said the thing to do is to pick a man and asked if DeLoach had anybody in mind. Mr. DeLoach told him that Mr. Hoover would have a better idea than he would.

Fortas said he was thinking of Ken Royall, who is a Johnson man and asked what DeLoach thought, who stated he had heard a few things about him. Fortas then asked DeLoach what he thought of Ross Malone, former President of the American Bar Association and DeLoach told him he knew Malone was friendly toward the Director and the Bureau. Fortas said there was another former President of the ABA in Richmond, Virginia, and DeLoach told him he was thinking of Louis Powell. DeLoach said that frankly, Powell is naive but is favorable toward the FBI. Fortas said he would talk to the President about these three men and if the Director had any ideas to let him know.

I told Mr. DeLoach I would, of course, be strongly inclined toward Ross Malone as I thought he would be a better man if they are going to name an arbitrator, although I did not see how they could work that around to supercede the Attorney General and the Solicitor General. I stated this means the whole thing then goes over to the fall term because an arbitrator will have to hold hearings and get our report.

- 2 -

Memorandum for Personal Files   June 14, 1966

        I told Mr. DeLoach I saw a memorandum which came through this morning from Ramsey Clark asking us to work with Rogovin in preparing the answers to these questions that the Court asked. I stated, of course, I did not intend to do that. I stated what I want to do is get our memorandum prepared. I stated there was one thing which I had not seen in the paper and was in the memorandum was the request for the identity of the attorneys in the Department who first learned of this microphone and the date, which was not covered in the press insofar as I saw. I stated that is a good point because the record shows we notified them in August, 1965, long before the Circuit Court had decided and certainly long before the case went to the Supreme Court. We notified the Attorney General with copies to Vinson and the Deputy.

        I told Mr. DeLoach that I thought if they felt it can be done by appointing an arbitrator, that's all right, that I knew the Department will not send up what we send over as they will distort and twist it.

        Mr. DeLoach stated he had mentioned this to Mr. Tolson, who was of the opinion we should go ahead and consider getting the material over to the Department as expeditiously as possible and I commented today, in fact. DeLoach said there was one thing he wanted to mention and that is, if we go ahead and send it over today and Katzenbach takes advantage of this and throws it out the window and gets one prepared and sends it up to the Supreme Court and the President calls him over and says he wants to appoint an arbitrator, Katzenbach will be in a position to say he has already answered the Supreme Court. I stated I thought that would put Katzenbach in bad with the President and the President would be outraged that Katzenbach had gone ahead and sent over a distorted and watered-down version of the facts and it might be the end of Katzenbach's days. I stated so far as getting facts out, we can probably work something along that line afterwards if Katzenbach pulls that trick. I stated we ought to get it on record and over to him and a copy to Watson for the President and if they go ahead and move on that this week and get it up without following what we say, I don't intend to change our verbiage at all; I flatly refuse and won't yield an inch insofar as substituting the phrase the "general Departmental authorization" which was the verbiage Katzenbach used originally and cut out. I am willing that be in the memorandum indicating this action was taken in line with general Departmental authorization that had prevailed for some years and had been reiterated by Attorney General Brownell, Rogers, and more specifically in writing by Attorney General Kennedy. I told Mr. DeLoach to get it in that way and if they are going to start an argument on that, I am just going to take an adament position that I will not change it and if they change it and send it up

- 3 -

Memorandum for Personal Files   June 14, 1966

they are falsifying the facts to the Supreme Court for which they will have to suffer the consequences. I stated in the meantime Fortas can try to get an arbitrator appointed.

       Mr. DeLoach stated there was one other angle; that Fortas referred to the Hoffa case and said he had disqualified himself insofar as the Hoffa case was concerned but he might get back in and asked DeLoach if he knew anything about electronic devices there and DeLoach said he did and that Kennedy had asked us to put one on Haggerty, the attorney in the case and Fortas was amazed and commented that now DeLoach had told him, he was going to qualify himself in that case again. I commented that they also had some man wired up who was dealing with Hoffa from New Orleans; that they put out orders to wire him up so there could be a recording of that although I did not know if it went through or whether he saw Hoffa or not, but I did know of the lawyer incident and that is damning itself.

       I stated that in the Black matter, to be certain to clarify the purpose for which it was put on, namely the crime syndicate in Las Vegas and it had nothing to do with the Bobby Baker case but dealt exclusively with the operations of the hoodlum element in Las Vegas. Mr. DeLoach stated he would have that in to the Director this morning.

       Mr. DeLoach commented he thought this meeting with Fortas was well worth it. I stated as it turned out, it was; that I was dubious as I don't know Fortas well myself, but I thought he would try to weasel out on the grounds it was improper for him as a member of the Court to even discuss the matter and then, of course, nothing could have been obtained, but he apparently is a more honest man than I gave him credit for. DeLoach stated that it boils down to the fact that he has to defend the President.

       I commented that I am surprised at Byron White disqualifying himself when he must remember the memorandum that went to him outlining in detail exactly what we were doing in the microphone situation and it was for the purpose of briefing Bobby Kennedy; now either he did or did not and if he didn't, he did not perform his duties as he should and I think he did and is trying to protect Bobby because Bobby had him appointed to the Supreme Court and of course, he is no doubt lined up with Bobby in connection with the Presidency. I stated

- 4 -

Memorandum for Personal Files   June 14, 1966

  Katzenbach was Bobby's choice for Attorney General and the President made a mistake in appointing him, particularly after Bobby asked him to and he is getting paid back now and I think rightly so by Katzenbach. It is more or less a doublecross.

    Mr. DeLoach stated Fortas asked him if there were any people in Justice who were loyal to Johnson and DeLoach told him one - Eddie Weisl, Jr. Mr. DeLoach stated Fortas asked about Ramsey Clark and DeLoach told him Clark sees no wrong in Kennedy. Fortas said the trouble with Ramsey Clark is he looks down in deep waters and sees nothing wrong with anybody and he is too dreamy. I stated that if the President asked me about him, I would say pretty much the same thing, that I think he is a nice fellow and an honest fellow, I think, but he supports Kennedy when any question comes up about the things Kennedy has done and he is a dreamy man and no man like that ought be appointed to be Attorney General at any time. I commented that like in the Giancana case in Chicago, it smells to high heavens that fellow Daley and the other fellow, who is probably a fence, were the two who interceded with Vinson and it resulted in the orders being issued to Hanrahan. I stated the thing that entered my mind in connection with seeing Fortas was that the Department went to see two Justices of the Supreme Court before they ordered the dropping of the Giancana case in Chicago and they were advised that if it came before the Supreme Court it would be reversed.

    Mr. DeLoach commented that we have got to fight to save our lives. I stated there was no question it is the greatest crisis we have had and I am not going, as I said when I had the conferences with Clark before, to be conciliatory but agreeable, but now it has been laid on the line and I will not agree to changing the phraseology. Mr. DeLoach stated that Fortas said it will be a continuing thing and not end with the Black Case but go into the Baker Case and the Hoffa Case and the FBI has to stand up right now. I stated anybody who has Edward Bennett Williams as their attorney can get Katzenbach to do anything.

    Mr. DeLoach stated Fortas mentioned this fellow Evans (Courtney A. Evans) and he told Fortas that I had instructed that he, DeLoach, call Evans and interview him and he told Fortas what Evans admitted. Fortas asked if the President knew Evans is working for Katzenbach and DeLoach told him the President did not. Fortas said the President ought to be told and if I would let DeLoach, DeLoach should tell the President right away because Evans, Sheridan and Bellino are birds of a feather; that he, Fortas, may be up on the Supreme Court but is aware of Evans' activities and knew very well of him even though he had never met him. I stated Evans is in a position where he is giving out a lot of money to groups and individuals around the country

- 5 -

Memorandum for Personal Files   June 14, 1966

in this Law Enforcement Assistance Act and it could be a powerful instrument in the political field of people that Bobby wants to have money given to or grants that are made. I stated they are proposing a big grant in New England which has an effect in Massachusetts and there Bobby or Edward Kennedy will get the credit for it. I stated if he would note, the releases on the grants of these sums of money are all made by Katzenbach and not by the White House where it should be made as it is a part of the over-all crime campaign the President is carrying on.

    I told Mr. DeLoach I would let Watson know about Evans and what a rat he is and how he denied these things until you pulled out the memorandum he himself had written and when confronted with that he then folded up. Mr. DeLoach stated he would reduce these to writing and I told him to make a memorandum on it and his conversation yesterday so we can have it in the confidential files at least. Mr. DeLoach stated he would get that material to me this morning.

John Edgar Hoover
Director

JEH:edm (1)

> 10/25/66
>
> MR. TOLSON:
>
> RE: CONVERSATION WITH JUSTICE FORTAS – ▓▓▓▓▓ MATTER; BLACK CASE
>
> For record purposes, Justice Fortas called ▓▓▓▓ at 10:30 this morning to express appreciation for the information the Director had me furnish him concerning the ▓▓▓▓▓▓▓▓ matter. Justice Fortas advised he agreed with the Director that no further action need be taken at this time. He stated he would get in touch with us in the event further inquiries should be made.
>
> While talking with Justice Fortas, I told him that perhaps he might consider the question I was about to ask a little off base; however, we were somewhat concerned about the Black case. I asked him if he knew when a decision would be handed down. He replied that there would be a decision probably on Monday a week (11/7/66). I asked him if we should prepare for the worst, inasmuch as he had previously advised me that the court was considering issuing a sweeping proclamation denouncing the use of electronic devices. He told me the court's thinking had changed somewhat concerning this matter.
>
> I asked him what he meant. He stated the court's decision would not be definitive. I asked him what he meant by that. He stated the court actually felt that the Black case and its various problems (meaning the microphone) should not be handled at Supreme Court level. I thanked the Justice for his information. It would seem that Justice Fortas undoubtedly meant that the Black case was to be remanded to the lower court.
>
> Pursuant to the Director's instructions, we are checking immediately to find out the identity of the judge who handled this matter in the lower court. A memorandum will be sent through on him just as soon as his identity is ascertained.

[1] Alexander Charns, *Cloak and Gavel. FBI Wiretaps, Bugs, Informers, and the Supreme Court* (Univ. of Illinois Press 1992), p. xv.

[2] U.S. Senate: Senate Select Committee to Study Governmental Operations with Respect to Intelligence Activities; See e.g., Church Committee Hearings, Vol. 6, FBI.

[3] HQ 190-13741-X (A FOIA request for FBI surveillance records about more than eighteen justices of the Supreme Court.)

[4] *Charns v. U.S. Dept. of Justice*, U.S.M.D.N.C. Civ. 89-208-D and 88-175-D (filed in Greensboro, NC in 1988 and 1989; Alexander Charns Papers, 1930-1990 (unc.edu) UNC-CH, Southern Historical Collection.

[5] Athan G. Theoharis and John Stewart Cox, *The Boss. J. Edgar Hoover and the Great American Inquisition*, (Temple Univ. Press 1988), pp. 94-96 (hereafter The Boss).

[6] Cartha D. "Deke" DeLoach, Hoover's FBI. The Inside Story by Hoover's Trusted Lieutenant (Regnery Publishing 1995), p. 62.

[7] The Boss, pp. 208-9; popular writer Anthony Summers, *Official and Confidential. The Secret Life of J. Edgar Hoover* (Putnam 1993), claimed a mobster and "Roy Cohn involved Edgar in [homosexual] orgies." Hoover was also said to dress in drag (253-54). However, the credibility of these stories has been questioned. Athan G. Theoharis, *J. Edgar Hoover, Sex and Crime: An Historical Antidote* (Ivan R. Dee 1995).

[8] Uncovered Papers Show Past Government Efforts to Drive Gays From Jobs - The New York Times (nytimes.com) 5/21/2014.

[9] See *Samahon v. Fed. Bureau of Investigation*, 40 F.Supp.3d 498 (E.D. Pa. 2014), p. 516 ("Furthermore, countless accounts have been published about the inner workings of Hoover's FBI, many of which discuss the agency's willingness to investigate high-profile individuals for unsubstantiated, improper, or personal reasons unconnected to the mission of the FBI.")

[10] David J. Garrow, *The FBI and Martin Luther King, Jr.* (Penguin 1983), pp. 125-127.

[11] Frank J. Donner, *The Age of Surveillance. The Aims and Methods of America's Political Intelligence* System (Vintage Books 1981), p. 116.

[12] I decided to not use George's full name. From the records I possess at this time, it is not clear how old George was at the time of his alleged sexual encounters with Abe Fortas. If they happened prior to 1964, he was a minor.

[13] Folder 71 Abe Fortas, J. Edgar Hoover's Official and Confidential (hereafter Hoover's "O&C") files, received in Charns v. U.S. Dept. of Justice, U.S.M.D.N.C. Civ. 89-208-D and 88-175-D; and a less redacted version received from The National Archives on 2/15/24, Record Group 65 Records of the Federal Bureau of Investigation

Official and Confidential Subject Files Entry UD 05D 14, Box 16@ 230/85/50/3 (hereafter "Folder 71, Hoover's 'O&C' files.") (see Appendix of documents at the end of this book.); Alexander Charns and Paul M. Green, "Playing the Information Game: How It Took Thirteen Years and Two Lawsuits to Get J. Edgar Hoover's Secret Supreme Court Sex Files," in *A Culture of Secrecy. The Government Versus the People's Right to Know*, Ed. Athan G. Theoharis (Univ. of Press of Kansas 1998), pp. 97-114 (Some conclusions in this essay were based on incomplete information on the available redacted records provided by the FBI. The 2024 release by The National Archives is more comprehensive and less redacted. One can see the difference by comparing the documents in the Appendix.)

[14] Folder 71, Abe Fortas, Hoover's "O&C" files, p. 6, The National Archives 2024 release.

[15] Neither Bartlett nor George is mentioned in the index to Laura Kalman, *Abe Fortas. A Biography* (Yale Univ. Press 1990); Ancestry.com listed both men as deceased.

[16] Carolyn E. Agger, Washington Post obituary [No. 11,] 1996" Wash. Post.

[17] Alexander Charns, *Cloak and Gavel. FBI Wiretaps, Bugs, Informers, and the Supreme Court* (Univ. of Illinois Press 1992), pp. 52-53 and endnotes.

[18] 372 U.S. 335 (1963).

[19] *Cloak and Gavel*, p. 52; n.56, p. 159 (Nat Hentoff, "Profile of Justice William Brennan," *The New Yorker*, 3/12/90, p. 62).

[20] *Cloak and Gavel*, p. 54.

[21] Folder 71, Abe Fortas Hoover's "O&C" files.

[22] Bruce Weber, NYT, 3/15/2013 (citing Tim Weiner, *Enemies: A History of the F.B.I.* DeLoach denied this allegation.

[23] Folder 71, Abe Fortas, Hoover's "O&C" files.

[24] Ibid.

[25] On 1/16/24, I re-requested this folder 71 about Fortas from the FBI under the FOIA to challenge their redactions. The first FBI response incorrectedly directed me to their on-line public repository of documents called The Vault. Folder 71 was not

among the FBI documents about Abe Fortas on their website. I appealed this denial of my rights under the FOIA to the U.S. Dept. of Justice. Paul M. Green referred me to The National Archives collection of FBI files. There I found and requested Folder 71 under the FOIA. It took the National Archives less than a week to release the FBI folder to me in a digital scan. This release had more unredacted information. The FBI release in my earlier litigation with the Bureau was incomplete and misleading.

[26] Folder 71, Abe Fortas, Hoover's "O&C" files.

[27] Ibid.

[28] *The Boss*, pp. 95, 331

[29] Laura Kalman, *Abe Fortas. A Biography* (Yale Univ. Press 1990), p.375 (hereafter *Abe Fortas*). A teenager spans the ages thirteen to nineteen. "Boy" implies a younger teen.

[30] If these conversations happened during the summer of 1969, Fortas had already resigned. At that point, he was citizen Fortas. He was of no use to Hoover or the FBI. *Abe Fortas*, p. 480, n. 87 and 88.

[31] Kourtney Geers, contributor, *Politico.com*, "In the Cloakroom and on the Floor," *Baker Text*, Bobby Baker interviews, June 2009 and May 2010, PDF page 193, Senate Historical Office, Washington, DC. [https://www.documentcloud.org/documents/836424-baker-text.html#document/]

[32] *Abe Fortas*, pp. 95-96.

[33] Cartha D. "Deke" DeLoach, *Hoover's FBI. The Inside Story by Hoover's Trusted Lieutenant*, (Regnery Publishing 1995).

[34] In addition to being considered offensive today, the word deviate as a noun is an archaic word with origins to the 15th century. The current word is deviant. "1630s, 'turn aside or wander from the (right) way' from Late Latin *deviatus*, past participle of *deviare* "to turn aside, turn out of the way," from Latin phrase *de via*, from *de* "off" (see de-) + *via* "way" (see **via**). Meaning 'take a different course, diverge, differ' is from 1690s. ... The noun meaning "sexual pervert" is attested from 1912. Also, from the 1630s." deviate | Etymology of deviate by etymonline [https://www.etymonline.com/word/deviate]

[35] https://www.eisenhowerlibrary.gov/sites/default/files/research/subject-guides/pdf/homosexuals-in-government-and-security.pdf

[36] Psychiatrists rule homosexuality no longer 'deviate' - UPI Archives

[37] https://www.oyez.org/cases/1966/440

[38] *Jacobs v. N.Y.*, 388 U.S. 431 (June 12, 1967).

[39] Brian L. Frye, *The Fortas Film Festival*, Columbia Law School Scholarship Archive, Studio for Law and Culture, p. 8; https://content.time.com/time/magazine/article/0,9171,838735,00.html

[40] *U.S. v. Black*, 282 F. Supp. 35, 37 (1968).

[41] "The Serv-U Man," Newsweek, 10/7/63; author interview with former FBI special agent Edward Scheidt, 10/14/90; author interview with Bubba Fountain, former congressional page, 10/9/90; *The Boss*, p. 346; Bureau files (Bufile) Headquarters (HQ) 62-98896 (Edward Bennett Williams); *Fred B. Black, Jr. v. U.S.*, Pet. For Writ of cert, O.T. 1965, No. 1029 (2/16/66), at 12a.

[42] Prior to becoming Solicitor General Thurgood Marshall, legal counsel for the NAACP, acted as an informant for the FBI passing on information about suspected communists in the civil rights movement. Alexander Charns, "My Hero Still," *Washington Post*, 12/16/1996; Juan Williams, *Thurgood Marshall. American Revolutionary* (Random House 1998), p. 280-1 (citing FBI Bufile HQ 100-111437).

[43] An indictment is the official charge document for felonies. It is issued by a grand jury after a finding of probable cause that a crime was committed.

[44] This chapter is based on *Cloak and Gavel* and endnotes for Chapter 3.

[45] SAC, WFO to Hoover, Julius Rosenberg et al., Espionage-R, 6/23/53; D.M. Ladd to Hoover, Julius Rosenberg et al., Espionage-R, 6/25/53, 62-27585-31; Alexander Charns, "FB-Eyed," *Durham Morning Herald*, 8/14/89; [Alexander Charns],"FBI kept Secret Files

on the Supreme Court," *NYT*, 8/21/89; Alexander Charns, "How the FBI Spied on the Supreme Court," *Washington Post*, 12/3/89.

[46] 357 U.S. 116 (1958).

[47] Valenti to Fortas, 1/29/66, Abe Fortas folder, box 195, WHCE, LBJ library; *Cloak and Gavel*, p. 55, n. 77, p. 160.

[48] This chapter is based upon *Cloak and Gavel* Chapter 4 and its endnotes.

[49] *Black v. U.S.*, 384 U.S. 983 (June 3, 1966).

[50] DeLoach to Tolson, 6/14/66, Fred Black folder, "O&C" files; Alexander Charns, "Gavelgate," *Southern Exposure* 18 Fall 1990); *Cloak and Gavel*, p. 57 and endnotes.

[51] Fred Black Folder, Hoover's "O&C" files; See *Samahon v. Fed. Bureau of Investigation*, 40 F.Supp.3d 498 (E.D. Pa. 2014), pp. 516-521. After reviewing an unredacted version of DeLoach's 1966 memo of his meeting with Fortas, the Federal judge found "Plaintiff has produced evidence of potentially improper conduct by the FBI; the *in camera* review has confirmed that disclosure exposes likely illegal or unethical conduct by at a minimum DeLoach and Justice Fortas; and the Government has conceded that there is a public interest served by disclosure." He also ruled that this 1966 memo did not contain evidence that Fortas had been blackmailed simply by its reference to George Hamilton who was dating LBJ's daughter at the time. The President had asked Fortas and DeLoach to dig up some dirt on him.

[52] DeLoach to author. 7/31/90.

[53] Fred Black Folder, Hoover's "O&C" files.

[54] 384 U.S. 436 (1966).

[55] Fred Black folder, Hoover's "O&C" files; see also T.J. McAndrews to Gale, Carmine Tramunti, a.k.a, et al., Interstate Transportation in Aid of Racketeering – Gambling, 12/7/65, 62-27585-NR, serial before 209.

[56] Fred Black folder, accession materials, Abe Fortas Papers (e.g. the preparation of the blind memo entitled "BLACK"); Douglas papers (Fortas talked Douglas out of writing an opinion about the powerful forces trying to knock him out of the case); see gen., Fred Black folder, Hoover's "O&C" files; (DeLoach tells Tolson and Hoover that Fortas said he was going to expose Robert Kennedy);

but see, in response to the author's 8/17/90 letter to Justice Brennan, concerning justice Fortas and the Black case, Justice Brennan wrote: "I regret that I have no information regarding Justice Fortas and the Black case."

[57] 347 U.S. 128 (1954).

[58] This chapter was based upon Hoover's "O&C" files, Fred Black folder, provided in *Charns v. DOJ*; Abe Fortas Papers, Sterling Memorial Library, Yale University; and *Cloak and Gavel*, chapters 5 - 6 and endnotes.

[59] Then called Cassius Clay.

[60] *U.S. v. Clay*, 430 F.2d 165-168 (5th Cir. 1970); *Cloak and Gavel*, p. 90 and n. 1, p. 170; Dr. Martin Luther King, Muhammad Ali and What Their Secret Friendship Teaches Us Today | The Nation https://www.thenation.com/article/archive/dr-martin-luther-king-muhammad-ali-and-what-their-secret-friendship-teaches-us-today/

[61] 388 U.S. 41 (1967); 389 U.S. 347 (1967).

[62] Senate Hearings on Fortas, p. 104.

[63] *Abe Fortas*, pp. 333-34.

[64] Bufile HQ 161-2860-59.

[65] DeLoach to Fortas, 2/16/67, "D" folder general, box 1, 1989 accession papers, Abe Fortas Papers; DeLoach to author, 11/13/90; White House "EYES ONLY" Memo from Larry Levinson to Jim Gaither, 8/17/68, File pertaining to Abe Fortas and Homer Thornberry, Chronological Files, 8/3/68-8/17/68, WHCF, LBJ Library. "Deke DeLoache (sic) was the 'point of contact' with Lou Nichols (V.P. of Schenley) a former FBI assistant director.

[66] Brian L. Frye, *The Fortas Film Festival*, Columbia Law School Scholarship Archive, Studio for Law and Culture.

[67] 393 U.S. 410 (1969).

[68] *Ibid.*

[69] 394 U.S. 165 (1969).

[70] 394 U.S. 576 (1969).

[71] Fortas memo to the Conference, 3/19/69, JMH Papers.

[72] *Tinker v. Des Moines*, 393 U.S. 503, 506 (1969).

[73] Hoover to Tolson et al., 4/23/69, 161-2860-NR after 75.

[74] DeLoach to author, 11/13/90; Did the FBI Try to Blackmail Supreme Court Justice Abe Fortas | History News Network (hnn.us) (undated) by Marc Stein. "Never proven, the allegations may have been made as a way for the FBI to threaten Fortas with exposure, encourage his resignation, or prevent his appointment as Chief Justice." Prof. Stein was told by the FBI that Folder 71 was "missing' by the time he made his 2004 FOIA request. Stein cites two documents printed in a 2009 J.J. Maloney web article Did J. Edgar Hoover Blackmail Justice Abe Fortas? Crime Magazine [Author's Note: As of March 8, 2024, I have not found evidence in the thousands of the FBI's files released to me, my interviews, or archival research, that Hoover or his Bureau were trying hound Fortas off the court. Fortas had been valuable and loyal to them. If he had become chief justice or remained a justice, they would have a powerful potential ally].

[75] Fact check: No evidence FBI organized Jan. 6 Capitol riot (usatoday.com) 6/25/21. Whether certain individuals were spurred to action by FBI informers is something that might take many years to determine.

[76] What is the Trump Mar-a-Lago case about and why is it significant? | Donald Trump | The Guardian 6/8/23

[77] "I" refers to FOIA requester and author Alex Charns; "we" refers to lawyers Alex Charns and Paul M. Green.

[78] Real X-Files, known within the FBI as "Do Not File," "June," "Personal & Confidential," and "Official & Confidential," may come to an agents attention for the first time only because they fall within the scope of an FOIA request; or they may have been jealously guarded for some time in a cache of sensitive records designated for special handling at the time they were created. Either way, the FBI's willingness to provide requesters with volumes of records responsive to their FOIA requests is not inconsistent with the simultaneous burial of one or more X-Files along the way. Some of the most sensitive records were kept in J. Edgar Hoover's Official & Confidential (O&C) files. Hoover kept these records in his office, separate from the ordinary FBI information indices. Some of these had been designated by him as "Personal & Confidential," and were slated for posthumous

destruction. The full record destruction plan was not carried out.

[79] The request went on: "including but not limited to FBI surveillance, bugging, wiretapping, efforts to force resignation, attempts to influence decision-making, attempts to gain copies of [Supreme C]ourt documents prior to public release, and use of Court employees as informants, directed at the court as a body or the above-named justices including but not limited to files and documents captioned in, or whose captions include... 'United States Supreme Court'... in the title. The request specifically includes 'main' and 'see reference' files [and the] ELSUR index." Charns to FBI, May 17, 1984, HQ 190-37116-21x2.

[80] FBI to Charns, September 4, 1984, 190-37116-29X3.

[81] For an explanation of the FBI's Central Records Systems, see e. g., *Federal Register* October 13, 1989, no.97, 42066 *et. seq.*, and the most recent FOI PA updates in the *Federal Register* and *Code of Federal Regulations.*

[82] FBI HQ file 62-27585, serial or document number 74 (62-27585-74).

[83] [Redacted] to Fee Waiver Committee, RE: FOIA request ... for records pertaining to the U.S. Supreme Court and [former named justices], August 30, 1984, 190-37116-29.

[84] Second declaration of Angus B Llewellyn, *Charns v. U.S. Department of Justice*, letter C-88-175-D (U.S. District Court for the Middle District of North Carolina, (March 21, 1990).

[85] *Cloak and Gavel*, p. 130.

[86] https://www.theguardian.com/us-news/2021/sep/14/brett-kavanaugh-fbi-investigation-documents

[87] https://www.whitehouse.senate.gov/news/release/fbi-director-confirms-agency-sent-tips-from-kavanaugh-tip-line-to-trump-white-house-without-investigation

[88] My FBI and litigation papers were donated to Alexander Charns Papers, 1930-1990 (unc.edu) UNC-CH, Southern Historical Collection and to Villanova Law Library www1.villanova.edu/villanova/law/library/specialcollections/

alexandercharnscollection.html

[89] If George was underage when Fortas allegedly had sexual encounters with him, Fortas is not a victim. He is someone who would have been prosecuted and impeached except for Hoover's blackmail scheme.

Made in the USA
Middletown, DE
08 April 2024